the **millennial mental health** toolbox

· · · · · · ·

Tips, Tools, and Handouts for Engaging Gen Y in Therapy

A Workbook for Clients and Clinicians Using

- Solution-Focused Therapy
- Cognitive Behavioral Therapy
- Mindfulness-Based Therapy

Goali Saedi Bocci, PhD

Copyright © 2020 Goali Saedi Bocci

Published by
PESI Publishing & Media
PESI, Inc.
3839 White Ave
Eau Claire, WI 54703

Cover: Amy Rubenzer
Editing: Jenessa Jackson, PhD
Layout: Amy Rubenzer & Bookmasters

ISBN: 9781683732839
Printed in the United States of America

PESI
Publishing
& Media
pesipublishing.com

About the Author

Goali Saedi Bocci, PhD is an award-winning licensed clinical psychologist in private practice, published author, millennial expert, TEDx speaker, educational trainer, and media personality. She earned a PhD in Clinical Psychology from the University of Notre Dame and completed her internship at the University of California, Berkeley, where she had the distinction of receiving a national honor when selected for the Outstanding Graduate Student/Intern award from APA's Division 17 Society of Counseling Psychology Section on College and University Counseling Centers. She completed her post-doctoral fellowship at Stanford University.

Dr. Saedi Bocci has been a columnist for *Psychology Today* for nearly a decade; her *Millennial Media* blog has garnered close to three million hits worldwide. She is the author of *The Social Media Workbook for Teens* (New Harbinger, 2019), the *Digital Detox Deck* (PESI Publishing and Media, 2019), *PhDiva* (Corby, 2015), and the upcoming *Positivity Workbook for Teens* (New Harbinger, 2020).

She is also a highly sought-after expert for top media outlets including *TIME*, *Newsweek*, *ABCNews*, *Chicago Tribune*, *Cosmopolitan*, *Refinery29*, *Elle*, *Glamour*, *Medium*, *Bustle*, and *Lifehacker*. Dr. Saedi Bocci has served as a recurring guest on the acclaimed morning television show *AM Northwest*, as well as *Good Morning San Diego*.

In addition to publishing in numerous APA peer-reviewed journals, Dr. Saedi Bocci has been serving as a reviewer for the *Psychology of Popular Media* journal since its inception in 2012. She currently serves as an adjunct professor at Pepperdine University's Graduate School of Education and Psychology. Dr. Saedi Bocci has also taught courses at Pacific University's School of Professional Psychology, the University of Notre Dame's Center for Social Concerns, and at Stanford University through the Department of Education for the Peer Bridge Program.

In 2013, Dr. Saedi Bocci gave a TEDx talk at Gunn High School in Palo Alto on the intersection between media, beauty, exoticization, and race in contemporary society. In 2018, she was awarded the highly selective Public Education Award from the Oregon Psychological Association. In 2019, she was a recipient of the Keep Oregon Well! Mental Health Heroes Award.

You can learn more about her work at www.drgoali.com.

Table of Contents

Part 1: Unique Challenges in Working With Millennials

Part 2: Problem Solving: Speedy Solutions for Millennials

Part 3: Managing Racing Thoughts and Rumination

Part 4: Grounding Frantic Energy

Acknowledgments

It is with deep gratitude that I express my thanks to all those who made this book possible. First, I'd like to thank my acquisitions editor (and fellow millennial) Karsyn Morse for sharing that spark of joy and enthusiasm in recognizing a deep need for a millennial resource such as this. Also, many thanks to my phenomenal content and line editor Jenessa Jackson for her amazing feedback and precision attention to detail that dare I say, was perfect. Thank you for rounding out our team of deeply invested millennials in bringing this resource to life! While it can be easy from my seat in the therapist's chair to witness trends and themes emerge among my millennial clients, it also takes an amazing publisher such as the PESI team to help bring such a project into fruition.

I'd also like to acknowledge my countless millennial clients, friends, and colleagues who have shown me the nuances of what it means to be living in the digital era. It is humbling to think that although millennials currently represent the last column in the Millennials vs. Past Generations Chart in Part 1 of this book, before we know it Generation Z and beyond will be making their mark on the world, and soon we will be our own version of the traditionalists. I genuinely hope and believe that our generation will make a lifelong impact for those yet to come, that we will be remembered for our strengths and compassion, and that we will ultimately leave the world in a better state.

As always, many thanks to my parents for sharing their love of the written word and the spirit of inquiry—the greatest gifts of all.

How one thanks a soul mate for existing, I'm not certain. No GRE flashcard word quite suffices. Looking out the window of my office, I see vibrant bushes of hydrangea blossoms planted with unconditional love. Thank you for that, and for allowing my endless pumpkin-spiced creations, which I solemnly swear are *not* a product of our millennial culture but are, in fact, necessary elements for research and writing. Thank you for seeing my promise and passion as a writer and making whatever sacrifices necessary, allowing the space for one of my great loves in our lives. In my life, I love you more.

Introduction

Millennials: They have been called the Me Generation, the Burnout Generation, and Generation Y. They make up one quarter of the U.S. population, having surpassed boomers as the largest generation to date. Commonly understood to have been born between the 1980s and 1996, millennials are also the most educated generation. They are the generation to complete college at the highest rate and to hold the most advanced degrees compared to any other. However, having grown up in the Great Recession, they are more likely to live with their parents for the first time in 130 years and experience financial distress and anxiety (American Psychiatric Association, 2017).

Millennials also lead the way in terms of their use of technology. Approximately 93% of millennials own smartphones, nearly 100% access the Internet, 19% access the Internet exclusively on their phones, and 86% use social media (Vogels, 2019). According to some statistics, millennials touch their smartphones 45 times a day, and 87% use two to three devices daily. They also spend roughly 25 hours per week online, with this figure growing by the year (Herosmyth, 2017).

Given the negative relationship between social media usage and emotional well-being, it should come as no surprise that low self-esteem, jealousy, and unhappiness abound among millennials. They are constantly faced with a barrage of highlight reels posted by peers in their social media newsfeeds. And they are often unfairly characterized as narcissists because of this very use of social media. However, as a generation who witnessed the birth of the Internet and the popularization of the selfie, technology is a natural platform by which millennials express and broadcast themselves.

Needless to say, millennials are a vibrant, dynamic group whose lives are often marked by an intense need to connect and feel as though they are a part of a larger community or social movement. However, the mental health community is only now catching up to understanding the unique needs of this generation. Although psychotherapy of the 1970s and 1980s was dubbed the "Golden Age of Psychotherapy"—with handsome insurance coverage and benefits—in today's health maintenance organization (HMO)-run system, that is no more. Given the limits that insurance companies place on the number of covered therapy sessions, coupled with millennials' limited financial resources, the face of psychotherapy is rapidly changing. In today's age, online apps sometimes stand in for therapy altogether, and tech-savvy consumers opt for online counseling that costs half the price and provides the convenience of therapy on the go.

While this certainly doesn't mean therapy is out and tech is in, it does mean that therapists do need to quickly get up to speed on what it means to work with the millennial client. The good news is millennials are open and—some might even argue—completely unfiltered. They are quick to open up, dive in, and learn tools to improve their mood. In fact, millennials have been dubbed the "Therapy Generation" for good reason. Having grown up in an era where parents often modeled going to therapy themselves, the stigma and barriers associated with reaching out for help have diminished significantly among this generation. Even more good news is that millennials are strong advocates for holistic well-being, as often evidenced by their social media feeds. Going to the gym, eating well, and taking care of their mind-body needs is something they readily advertise to friends and the world at large. Therefore, don't be surprised if a photo of your office door ends up on a millennial's Snapchat!

A MILLENNIAL PERSPECTIVE

As a millennial and psychologist, it has been fascinating to witness and be a part of this perplexing group. I joined Facebook after much peer pressure following a summer undergraduate psychology institute held at Vanderbilt University years ago. The idea was that we could keep in touch over the years and see how one another's careers progressed. Over time, of course, like all millennials, my Facebook "friends" group slowly started including acquaintances from high school, long-lost cousins, elementary school friends, and my high school French teacher. Graduate school colleagues, college professors, and random apartment neighbors then added on to the growing list. My parents also joined the bandwagon, adding yet another element of complexity when they questioned the meaning behind my posts, or why I was photographed with one person or another.

Naturally, life became akin to the popular Facebook status: *complicated*. Over the years, my relationship with this platform fluctuated—taking yearlong hiatuses, only to be thrilled to reconnect with colleagues shortly later. But then the hassles of managing privacy settings, avoiding potential therapy clients, and managing who could see what posts became a part-time job. The incessant photos of Hawaiian vacations from five years back (often called *throwbacks*), and endless self-promotion and multi-level-marketing plugs did me in for good.

Like most millennials, I logically understood these were what are colloquially described as *humble brags*, but emotionally it was harder to disconnect. I logically understood what it was like to want to show off one's major accomplishments while still appearing grounded. After all, getting your PhD can be a decade-long feat, and finally saving up for that dream vacation is something you want to shout from the rooftops. But we all have our limits in how much bragging (and sometimes even worse, constant complaining) we can take.

As a psychologist, I could see the invasive and pernicious subconscious influence of constantly being bombarded by the images, emotions, and thoughts of others. Was I craving pumpkin spice because it was really how I felt, or was I "vibing" off the energy of others? Where did the line between my own identity and groupthink diverge?

When everyone is posting about politics on social media, it is natural to join the bandwagon. But are you slowly turning into a political advocate or just mimicking the behaviors of others? Are you posting a photo of yourself with the "I voted" sticker to add another post to your social media feed, or are you trying to fit in? Many millennials are unaware of just how much of their day-to-day lives is a reaction to the mass stimuli they are exposed to on a regular basis.

WHO IS THIS BOOK FOR?

As a psychologist who is ever on the hunt for the right resources for my therapy clients, this book was written with two primary audiences in mind: millennials and the clinicians helping them. From my therapist hat, I know all too well how well-intentioned resources can wind up poorly executed. Some resources may provide plentiful handouts but fail to provide any substantive backing to explain the logistics. Especially for beginning therapists or those venturing into new therapeutic modalities for the first time, it can be intimidating to figure out how best to explain a tool and have clients actually return the following week having practiced it.

From the perspective of an often embarrassingly impatient millennial myself, I also understand the need for immediate applicability and, frankly, skimmability! I don't want to be bothered with excessively long and drawn-out explanations, but I also want clarity. I want to know how much time something will take me and what I am getting out of it. Of course, with this attitude, I also know I need to continue practicing patience and mindfulness (discussed in Part 4 of this book), and that I need to take my own advice once in a while and actually slow down and breathe.

Throughout this workbook, I draw on a host of evidence-based tools from an array of therapeutic modalities aimed at everything from common maladies (e.g., sleep concerns and everyday stress) to troublesome behaviors and thought patterns (e.g., procrastination and perfectionism) that run rampant among millennials. By providing millennials and clinicians with the tools needed to engage a generation that is unlike any other, it is my hope that this book will assist you in empowering millennials to move away from simply surviving the daily grind to truly thriving. Some millennials will just need a few tools and tricks to help them move from burnout to standout when it comes to their careers. Others will simply need a nudge to go from feeling lonely and isolated to feeling connected and content. Whatever the goal at hand may be, it is my hope that this resource can help them get back on track.

HOW TO USE THIS BOOK

This workbook is divided into four primary sections. **Part 1** discusses the unique challenges in working with millennials, and it also gives you various tips to navigate the complexities associated with the constant technological interference they experience in their daily lives. As feeling connected is so important to this generation, becoming familiar with their lexicon can be particularly beneficial for establishing a strong therapeutic alliance. Just as millennials regularly shop online for goods and services, their perusal of therapists is similar. They seek fit and understanding. If you are a millennial reading this section, you may still find this topic to be instructive and informative, as it can be validating to read about the similarities of your challenges in the context of your generation.

Part 2 dives into the clinical essentials. Given that millennials themselves are so diverse and varied, an eclectic approach is key. Not all millennials will readily hop onto the mindfulness train, nor will they immediately take to one purist approach to psychotherapy. As solution-focused therapy (SFT) is excellent for "quick-fixes," ranging from insomnia and procrastination to erratic eating patterns, tools in this arena are presented first. Given that millennials are often strapped for time and cash, effective psychotherapy needs to be brief and offer solutions promptly. This does not mean more extensive process-based work cannot be done. It's simply that millennials are used to immediacy, so offering initial tips and tools that can help them on a day-to-day basis is a strong way to establish trust, usefulness, and continuity.

In my own psychotherapy work with millennials, I spend a good amount of time in processing early on and throughout the work, but I also balance this with handouts and tools from the first session and sprinkle in these interventions throughout. I attempt to give them enough concrete tools that they feel they are making tangible progress without overwhelming them with countless handouts that they do not always have time for. While there may be interrupted periods of time when millennials cease treatment due to finances, work transitions, or other reasons, they are highly resourceful and can track you down (which has always thrilled me as I love hearing what old clients have been up to and how I can help them meet their goals now). The tools I provide in this workbook can easily be used by millennials in the interim to keep up their overall well-being.

Part 3 discusses the use of cognitive behavioral therapy (CBT) to help millennials manage racing thoughts and rumination. Millennials often instantly connect with concepts such as cognitive distortions given how quickly they intake information and make snap judgments. Further, given that this generation tends to gravitate toward unhealthy coping mechanisms (e.g., binge drinking and casual sexual encounters that lead to later regret), a variety of healthy coping tools are provided. Millennials in the digital era can also struggle with discerning their own emotions, as well as that of others. Therefore, tools focused on understanding emotions are also included in this section.

Finally, **Part 4** discusses how millennials can use mindfulness-based therapy (MBT) to slow down and manage restless energy. Mindfulness has been steadily gaining popularity and acceptance among millennials and other generations at large. The concepts of meditation and yoga are far less intimidating or eccentric sounding as they were only several decades ago. The tremendous amount of research that's been done in this domain has somewhat Westernized these ancient practices, making them more accessible to those seeking these tools for well-being purposes.

In Parts 2 through 4 of this book, you will find a therapist overview section that presents a brief summary of each corresponding tool I have presented, as well as an accompanying client worksheet, handout, or activity. To make this workbook as accessible as possible, though, each tool begins with a brief primer that allow these resources to stand on their own so clients don't have to read a lengthy therapist explanation beforehand.

Each tool features a suggested duration (ranging from 1 minute to 90 minutes), frequency (daily, weekly, as needed), and level of difficulty (easy, moderate, challenging). These indicators can be helpful for clients in terms of planning how much time and effort may be needed for each activity. For example, daily 5-minute activities that are relatively easy can be a breeze for clients to integrate early on in the therapy process. In contrast, weekly 40-minute activities that are more challenging may be best saved for later on in the therapy process or simply when the client is feeling less frantic and more in charge of their lives. Being mindful of a client's emotional bandwidth can also aid therapists in determining which activities might be most appropriate depending on difficulty level and time commitment.

Of course, clinicians may choose to skip around this book in an order that best meets the needs of their clients. The rationale behind the presented layout is that once clinicians understand the millennial client, they can better help them by first offering interventions that support millennials' daily lives (SFT), and then move onto providing them with tools to calm their ruminating thoughts (CBT), and finally encourage them to try interventions that provide grounding and peace (MBT).

Additionally, in an effort to provide maximal tools and learning opportunities, bonus tips are provided throughout. Look for these **BONUS** tip icons throughout this workbook:

Tech Tip: As digital natives, millennials are comfortable with a range of technologies, many of which often start with an "i" prefix. Whether a phone, tablet, e-reader, music device, wearable (watch or jewelry that senses movement), desktop, or streaming device (e.g., Netflix®, YouTube), millennials are truly immersed in technology. These tips will help clarify what some of those dense jungle of cords mean and pertain to.

Social Media Tip: Social media is integrated into the fabric of many millennials' lives. Tips describing the nuances and nitty gritty of these platforms will be delineated throughout the workbook. Whether clients are using Facebook, Instagram, or Snapchat, these social media tools have certainly created their own lexicon.

Terminology Tip: Millennials love their trendy lingo. But this can also leave their therapist and others behind when they use unfamiliar terms. Throughout this workbook, these tips will integrate common terms you might hear your millennial client using.

In-Session Tip: Moving from the theoretical to applied aspect of therapy can sometimes feel vague and confusing. In-Session tips aim to further integrate the tips and tools you are learning into practical and applied uses directly in the therapy office.

Millennial Vignette: Sometimes, the best way to learn can be through the use of examples. Throughout this workbook, I have included several vignettes that describe millennials struggling with a host of issues and highlight means of working with them to improve their mental health.

Part 1

unique challenges in
working with
millennials

Who Are Millennials?

Tip #1 | Understanding Millennials vs. Other Generations

Every time I walk into a coffee shop, I am instantly struck by just how different millennials can be from past generations. I often observe them waiting around with their heads bent forward and their thumbs rapidly scrolling through their feed. They often stand, rarely sit, and hastily rush off after grabbing their order. This is in stark contrast to older generations who are often casually seated with their newspapers strewn about a large table, leisurely enjoying a cup of coffee. Technology has drastically impacted norms among millennials, and it has increased 24/7 work expectations, the pressure to always be accessible, and challenges with truly slowing down.

According to research from the U.S. Chamber of Commerce (2012), millennials are the most studied generation of all time. Given that there are over 80 million individuals that comprise this generation, there is plenty of data regarding their unique strengths, contradictions, and growth edges. Perhaps one of the most fascinating ways to understand millennials is by comparing and contrasting them with previous generations.

In the **Millennials vs. Past Generations** chart that follows, consider your own generational background, as well as that of your parents, grandparents, and even influential figures in history. This can help to open up your eyes to the exquisitely complicated (and connected) world of millennials.

In-Session Tip:
Consider discussing this chart with your millennial client in relation to parents, work supervisors, or even the therapeutic reliance. Millennials highly value honesty and transparency, and they are likely to respond positively to a frank discussion of the differences between the therapist and themselves or other close ones in their lives.

Millennials vs. Past Generations

	Traditionalists	Baby Boomers	Generation X	Millennials
Birth Years	1900-1945	1946-1964	1965-1980	1981-1996
Famous People	Audrey Hepburn, Martha Stewart, Bob Dole, JFK, Robert De Niro, John Glenn, Helen Mirren	Princess Diana, Bono, Bill Gates, Bill and Hillary Clinton, Deepak Chopra, Katie Couric	J.K. Rowling, Leonardo DiCaprio, Michael Jordan, Barack Obama, Tiger Woods	Kate Middleton, Mark Zuckerberg, Beyoncé, Usain Bolt, Michael Phelps
Other Names	Silent Generation, Forgotten Generation, Maturists	"Me" Generation	Gen X, Xers, Post Boomers	Generation Y, Gen Y, Echo Boomers
Influences	WWII, Korean War, Great Depression, New Deal, Space Age/NASA, Stock market crash	Civil rights movement, Vietnam War, Sexual revolution, Cold War/Russia, Space travel	Watergate, Energy crisis, Dual-income families vs. single parents, First latchkey kids, Increased divorce rate	School shootings, 9/11, AIDS, Terrorism, Economic recession, Children of divorce, More sheltered than children of past generations, First generation of children with schedules
Core Values	Discipline, Delaying gratification, Adherence to rules, Hard work, Patriotism, Trust in government	Anti-war, Anti-government, Extreme loyalty to their children, Involvement, Optimism, Team-orientation	Diversity, Independence, Pragmatism, Self-reliance, Balance, Skepticism/Cynicism, Suspicion of boomer values, Fun	Achievement, Diversity, Civic duty, Education, Extreme fun, Tolerance of others, Competitiveness, Self-confidence, Tech-savviness, Optimism, Realism
Attributes	Believe in sacrifice and a strong work ethic, Honorable, Conservative, Thrifty	Believe in consumerism, Challenge authority, Competitive, Live to work, Loyal to career and employers	Free agents, Ignore leadership, Skeptical of institutions, Work to live, Adaptable	Eager to spend money, Diversity-focused, Individualistic but team-oriented, Have not lived without computers, Give respect for competency (not titles), Parents advocated for them and indulged them
Family Experience	Traditional, Nuclear	Stay-at-home mothers, "Beaver Cleaver" family	First generation of "day care" kids, Working moms	Merged families, Considered "coddled" by parents, schools, and organizations (e.g., participation trophies)
Education	A dream	A birthright	A way to get there	An incredible expense
Focus	Tasks	Relationships and results	Tasks and results	Global and networked
Technology Is….	The Hoover Dam	The microwave	What you hold in your hand (e.g., cell phones, tablets)	Ethereal and intangible
Communications & Media	Rotary phones, Writing memos	Touch-tone phones	Cell phones	Internet, camera phones, email

Tip #2 Me Generation, Burnout Generation: Avoiding Misunderstandings About Millennials

As a clinician, your initial reactions to working with millennials may be mixed depending upon your own demographic background. Much like many young clinicians who fear working with the elderly due a lack of knowledge or direct experience, millennials can be a welcome or intimidating group to work with. Due to their propensity toward using their own slang, terminology, and popular culture references, connecting with millennials may initially seem challenging.

Furthermore, the numerous negative stereotypes about this generation do not help in enhancing the therapeutic relationship, especially among clinicians who may be boomers or GenXers. Of course, while therapists are often open-minded and check their stereotypes at the door, it is still important to be aware of the major negative descriptors attributed to this group. After all, whether in the workplace or at home, these clients may be susceptible to being seen through these common millennial stereotypes. The following list includes many of the negatively skewed terms used to describe millennials. It is important to note that some are in fact true and based off of research (e.g., the Loneliest Generation), whereas others include value judgements (e.g., the Me Generation).

- **Me Generation**: Due to the boom of social media and technology, millennials are seen as the generation that loves to self-promote. According to the National Institutes of Health, millennials are three times more likely to have narcissistic personality disorder relative to boomers (Stinson et al., 2008).

- **Loneliest Generation**: An almost ironic result of the social media movement is that incessant connection mediated through devices is decreasing face-to-face connections. It is easier than ever for millennials to cancel plans via text message, whereas decades ago, a phone call was necessary, making it more personal (and making it less likely for people to "flake" on plans). Research indicates 30% of millennials report constant feelings of loneliness relative to 20% of Gen Xers and 15% of boomers.

- **Broke Generation**: As a result of growing up during the Great Recession, which provided little economic opportunities for building wealth, the average net worth of millennials is $8,000.

- **Indebted Generation**: Largely due to student loan debt, millennials have accumulated over one trillion dollars in debt, representing a rise of 22% in the last five years.

- **Rental Generation**: A natural outgrowth of minimal financial resources, millennials are more likely to rent apartments than own homes and even rent cars or use rideshare services. Everything from clothing to furniture to office space is now being rented by millennials.

- **Burnout Generation**: As a result of long hours, little pay, and minimal private spaces of their own, it is no surprise that millennials are burned out. Many work multiple side jobs to supplement their income, and mental health concerns have skyrocketed among this generation.

- **Netflix Generation**: As a means of coping, "binge-watching" is common among this generation. Further, streaming technologies are particularly popular among millennials due to cost efficiency and immediacy.

- **Snowflake Generation**: Often criticized as having difficulty when it comes to receiving negative feedback, many millennials have been dubbed as "snowflakes" who see themselves as unique and in need of more praise than constructive feedback.

After reading through this list, it can help to check your reactions to and experiences of millennials in your own life. While headlines often tout millennials as lazy or entitled, many of these stories are exaggerated and leave out some of the critical antecedents to their lived experiences. Social media has been a mixed blessing and curse for millennials, as it has aggrandized extravagant and picture-perfect lifestyles that an economic recession makes an impossibility. Millennials are constantly living a life in an altered reality state, seeing false images plastered on their social media feeds every day without the reminder that many of these images are not real. Gen Xers may have grown up with billboards and magazines touting images of airbrushed models and lifestyles, but that is a far cry from today's bombardment of toxic social media imagery.

Tip #3   Focusing on Millennial Strengths

While many descriptors of millennials are often negatively skewed, the reality is that this generation is also one of the most educated and socially conscious groups to date. Reframing and shifting the focus to the unique positive attributes of this cohort is beneficial both for clients and therapists alike. Past research has indicated that the simple act of reviewing a client's positive characteristics before a psychotherapy session can boost the therapeutic alliance, improve treatment outcomes, and facilitate the client's sense of mastery (Flückiger & Grosse Holtforth, 2008). Therefore, it can be important to consider alternative descriptors that have been given to millennials:

- **Most Educated Generation**: According to research conducted by the Pew Research Center (2019), 39% of millennials possess a bachelor's degree or higher in comparison to 29% of Gen Xers and 25% of boomers.

- **Most Diverse Generation**: Approximately 43% of millennials are a member of a minority group (Pew Research Center, 2014). Due to immigration from Asian and Latin American nations, interracial marriages, and fertility patterns, millennials are currently the most diverse generation to date (although early data suggests Generation Z may be closing in on this statistic).

- **Wellness Generation**: Because millennials value health and fitness, some have dubbed them the "wellness generation." They are likely to exercise more, smoke less, and eat healthier. The rise of social media has likely also fueled this trend, with influencers and food bloggers inspiring healthy lifestyles and eating. Juicing, detoxing, and dietary choices such as veganism, paleo, and keto have surged in popularity among this group.

- **Therapy Generation**: Having grown up with parents who more openly attended therapy and in an era where there was greater destigmatization of such services, this generation is eager to engage in self-improvement and manage their mental health. This is positive news given the rise in anxiety, depression, and burnout in this generation. Further, many celebrity and social media figures have openly discussed their own mental health struggles, which has opened the door for greater acceptance and openness toward therapy in this generation.

In addition to these generational descriptors, additional terms used to positively encapsulate millennials include the following:

- Tech-savvy
- Resourceful
- Zero intolerance
- Multitaskers

- Eco-conscious
- Team player
- Activist
- Enthusiastic

Being aware of millennial strengths is key. As you continue working with this population, consider adding some of your own observations to the list so you can have a handy resource for your own situational reframes. For example, when millennials cancel an appointment, it may be natural to turn toward stereotypes, such as "They are so flaky!" On the flip side, millennials can be quite adaptable and open to unconventional appointment times (e.g., meeting for a brief virtual session) as a means of balancing their constantly shifting priorities. It has been my experience that millennial clients can be a true joy to work with, as they can be highly empathic, flexible, and understanding, not only in their approach to the logistics of therapy but to the greater therapeutic concerns at large.

Millennials in the Workplace

Tip #4 | Understanding Millennial Trends in the Workforce

Millennials are the most researched generation to date, and studies on their work habits are among the most discussed findings. As millennials make up the largest portion of the workforce and are estimated to comprise 50% of the labor force in the coming years, understanding how this group functions is key. According to a recent Gallup poll, millennials are the least engaged generation in the workforce, with only 29% reporting that they are engaged (versus 55% not engaged and 16% actively disengaged). They also change jobs more frequently than any other generation in history, and this millennial turnover costs the U.S. economy an estimated $30.5 billion annually (Emmons, 2018).

These numbers are concerning to say the least, but also understandable. If you recall from Tip #1, millennials are individualistic but also team-oriented and civic-minded. For millennials, their concern is more with having a vocation than a job. They want meaning and impact, and they don't want to waste any time getting there. This is unlike boomers who may have worked the same job for over 30 years without any passion or true investment in the company other than their pension plans. For millennials with extremely uncertain economic futures (will Social Security even exist by the time they retire?), being engaged in the here and now is critical. Further, high debt loads, unemployment, and even under-employment have diminished many millennials' upward mobility. It is not uncommon to hear of millennial therapy clients vying for barista jobs with a bachelor's degree in hand.

Additionally, the way that millennials engage with technology in the workplace is like no other given that they grew up with the Internet. In fact, while most Americans access the Internet through their computers, the overwhelming majority of millennials do so through their phone, which is more than any other generation. Instead of using written memos to record missed messages at work—as the traditionalists did—millennials are likely to communicate via direct text message today. Escaping one's boss may be a true impossibility, and boundaries can quickly be crossed as technology allows for constant intrusions into the personal non-work hours in a millennial's life. As a result, millennials are more prone to burnout as technology has made 24/7 availability more accessible than ever.

So what can we do to help millennials feel more engaged and motivated in the workforce? Factors such as money, job security, paid time off, and flexibility are key, but only when millennials are initially looking for a job. To increase the likelihood they will stay in a position (and be more loyal to their work and to the company), millennials must feel like their job gives them a sense of purpose and meaning. In addition, the following factors may reduce job turnover: a pay increase or bonus, a new challenge or promotion, better work-life balance, a clear career path, and recognition by managers and colleagues (ManpowerGroup, 2016). The positive takeaway here is that millennials are looking for new challenges and opportunities rather than an escape from their current employment situation. Millennials want more than a paycheck; they want purpose (Gallup, 2016).

As a clinician supporting a millennial client, workplace issues can be a common theme, as can job dissatisfaction or burnout. While negative stereotypes may lead clinicians to point toward entitlement or other similar factors contributing to client work dissatisfaction, further assessment of the situation can be beneficial. From there, a number of clear clinical issues may emerge that the therapist can help the client actively work on. Common issues and solutions worth working toward may include:

Work Issue	Therapy Solutions/Processing Points
Feeling lost or hopeless at work	Process ways to approach their boss or mentor to get feedback or receive more challenging tasks
Feeling overworked or burned out	Set boundaries with technology (e.g., if using two phones, then silence work cell after-hours), and don't work evenings or weekends
Stressors around commute	Advocate for telecommuting and working from home one day per week
No friends at work or interpersonal concerns	Discuss moving teams, networking, or moving office locations
Financial concerns	Consider how to ask for a raise, take on new responsibilities with more pay, or further education to advance to leadership

As millennials become a more dominant force in the workplace over time, learning to support them and understand their key concerns is a critical part of improving their overall well-being.

It can better equip therapists in discussing vocational, career, and long-term goals throughout the counseling process.

Millennial Vignette:
I once worked with a male client from a historically underprivileged group who was working himself into the ground. He was working long hours with tremendous amounts of travel on short notice. His primary symptoms were manifesting physically as he was often exhausted, losing weight, and struggling in interpersonal relationships. We worked on setting boundaries the best he could while also focusing on the future. What was next? Was the company going to burn him out and then move onto the next employee who was going to be treated the same way? We focused on setting healthier dietary goals, incorporating exercise into his routine, and practicing stress management techniques, along with improving communication skills at work. At the backdrop of all of this was a focus on graduate school programs that might provide funding and a way to climb the corporate ladder.

Understanding Technology

It is truly incredible how much communication mediums have evolved in such a short period of time. In fact, the change has been so rapid that it would not be unfathomable for Morse code to become trendy in the next several decades. The speed of change in communication methods and preferences among millennials is both positive and negative. On the one hand, it is highly efficient. On the other hand, it can lead to all communication being mediated through technology and the loss of voice, charm, and sincerity. As anyone who has had a miscommunication occur via text message can attest, it is clear that even a word such as "okay" can be fully loaded. To some, it's simply "sounds great," whereas to others, it means "if I have to, I'll go along with it."

Email can allow for greater depth of communication relative to shorter messages via text or other messaging mediums, but much still gets lost in translation. While most work communications for millennials involve email in favor of phone calls, this does not mean millennials are masters of email by any means. In fact, author Jocelyn Glei (2016) discusses the vast problems inherent in this technology. She shares that while several decades ago, communication involved the effort of putting a stamp on an envelope and dropping it in the mail, nowadays anyone with an Internet connection has immediate access to any individual. There is literally no barrier to entry. This equates to inboxes with thousands of unopened messages, ranging from LISTSERVS® that subscribed you for that one-time purchase you made to even more random spam.

A few tips that might help you or your millennial client better manage email:

- *Autoresponders are your friend*. Use them before-hours, after-hours, on weekends, and definitely when on vacation. Even use them to say you'll get back to the sender when you have more time (i.e., don't expect an immediate response!).

- *Use email templates*. Glei provides several examples in her book, but the gist is the same. If you always get emails on the same topics or themes, come up with a draft, change the details, and copy and paste. This is much faster and more efficient than typing up different versions of the same messages every week.

- *Unsubscribe*. It might be a pain, but spend a day and actually go through the effort of unsubscribing from each of those pesky LISTSERVS you ended up on, and even block them for more assurance. You'll be amazed how much better you feel.

- *File, file, file*. Create folders, subfolders, or color code. Do whatever you need to do to organize it all. You can even have a "read later" file just to clean things up.

- ***Slow things dooowwwnnn.*** Slowing down isn't popular in the workplace, but email can become so cumbersome that you never get anything done on your to-do list because you are constantly managing everything that comes up. Be polite and be prompt, but set an expectation of at least one response per 24-hour window on non-urgent tasks and requests.

- ***Check email no more than two or three times per day.*** Many executives and CEOs swear by a twice-a-day email check. First thing in the morning, they set aside some time to exercise, meditate, eat a healthy breakfast, and read the paper. *Then* they check email and get back to others. They do a solid block of work for several hours and then do another check later in the day or evening to wrap up the emails for the day. Totally reasonable and keeps distractions at bay.

In-Session Tip:

It is important for the therapeutic work to address email as it pertains to communication with the therapist. Many therapists have a no-email policy (I use a secure messaging system through my billing and scheduling provider), whereas others send appointment notifications to emails that are never even checked. On the other hand, some clients may abuse relaxed email policies by sending pages of content that can create boundary concerns. Whatever your (and your millennial client's) stance is on email, it is worth discussing and processing at the outset of therapy before greater problems arise.

Tip #6 | Texting and Health Hazards

The average person sends or receives a staggering 50 text messages a day (Bratskeir, 2017). As ubiquitous as texting and messaging is for millennials, the associated health ramifications often go unnoticed. While it can be common for millennials to brush off any intimation that their digital habits are harmful to their well-being, research indicates that a whole host of new ailments are associated with texting and excess time on smartphones and other related devices. These include but are not limited to:

- Radiation exposure
- "Text neck"
- Hand/wrist strain
- Sleep disturbance
- Eye strain

- Driving accidents
- Walking accidents
- Joint pain
- Occipital neuralgia

According to the National Safety Council, pedestrian deaths increased for the first time since 1990 with distracted walking (and driving) being a possible contributor to this statistic (Chadra, 2016). Not only is technology highly distracting for clients on the road, but it also distracts them in the workplace and throughout their daily lives. It results in sleep disturbance due to excessive light exposure, and in severe cases, neurological damage can result due to excessive strain put on the spine resulting from phone usage. The incidence of occipital neuralgia, which involves compressed or damaged occipital nerves, has also skyrocketed since the introduction of smartphones (Estes, 2018).

Given these concerns, when conducting an intake assessment with millennial clients, it is important to be aware of physical ailments and other conditions that could be impacted by technology usage. Whether it is unexplained headaches, back pain, or other concerns, a referral to a physician for a medical check-up can prove useful.

In-Session Tip:

As will be noted throughout this workbook, it is highly recommended that you encourage millennials to have time away from their devices. The therapy hour itself can be instructive toward this end. If you see messages constantly coming through and lighting up your client's phone while they are in session, you might encourage them to put the phone away or out of sight. Emphasize the importance of the therapy hour being a full focus on them with no distractions. When a phone is even visible on a table during a conversation, level of disclosure can go down (Ward et al., 2017). For therapy, this finding is critical and brings home the importance of time off of devices.

Terminology Tip:

Within the domain of texting, the notion of "textationships" is one worth being aware of. Among single millennials, there can be plentiful terminology to elucidate the nature of relationships and how technology plays into things. Many times, a desired relationship may turn into a textationships when two individuals spend more time communicating virtually rather than IRL (in real life). This can be the cause of frustration for some and be a means of avoidance for others. Furthermore, the rules and decorum involving texting can quickly become unclear and muddy. Encourage millennials to move from their devices (and away from relationships mediated through technology) and to shift toward live conversations instead (even if they are on FaceTime!®).

Tip #7 | Embracing Technology in Clinical Practice

For any modern therapist, embracing technology in clinical practice can be integral to staying connected to clients. Too many times, therapists may insist on not having a web presence, using text message reminder systems, or other simple tools that can improve the therapy process for clients. Having worked with a supervisor not too long ago who wrote out receipts for clients on a carbon paper system, and working at clinics where charts were all paper, I quickly came to see embracing technological advances can not only improve security and privacy, but also help organization and record-keeping. A few "modern" advances to consider integrating into your practice include:

- *Electronic Records Systems (EHR, EMR)*: While many providers associate electronic records with the complicated and sometimes bizarre systems in hospital and bigger clinics, dozens of simple-to-use systems have emerged for the purposes of private practitioners.

- *Client Portals*: It sounds alien, but it truly is not. Client portals allow for short messages back and forth to coordinate appointment times and other minor details. Many systems that use portals are mobile-enabled, which makes clients feel like they can text their therapist (without the boundary violation). In contrast to email communication, it is also secure.

- *Electronic Billing Systems*: Whether using a card reader, an online "shopping cart," or an integrated charting, scheduling, and billing system, moving payments to the online domain goes a long way in keeping payments secure and your sanity intact. No more spreadsheets tracking the five different ways you generate income. Whether it is just for co-pays or insurance deposits (which allow direct deposits instead of paper checks), this can keep things much cleaner. Perhaps most importantly, it keeps therapy focused on the heart of the matter rather than ending each session with an awkward business-like exchange.

- *Electronic Scheduling Systems*: Millennials go online to do anything from booking a haircut to getting groceries delivered through the click of a mouse, and they may prefer the ease of being able to schedule therapy sessions the same way. Electronic scheduling systems allow you to retain the ability to directly schedule some people yourself, but it also gives clients autonomy in scheduling, which can be highly empowering.

- *Automatic Reminders:* Don't you appreciate it when you have a dentist appointment coming up and you get a reminder 24 or 48 hours in advance? Your clients feel the same way about therapy appointments.

Tech Tip:
The same welcoming spirit toward embracing technology in clinical practice can extend to using technology in therapy practice. Ever do a clinical rotation using biofeedback and sensors? You may have been amazed to see how your breathing and heart rate came alive on a screen. Such fancy technology isn't needed in daily practice, but embracing the use of apps (many are free) can go a long ways in supporting your therapy work. A few apps to learn more about and consider integrating into your practice include:

- *Mood trackers*: not just for CBT practitioners!
- *Meditation apps*: for teaching guided meditations and tracking silent meditations
- *Period tracker apps*: for clients tracking the relationship between mood and their menstrual cycle
- *Fitness apps*: for teaching workout routines, or connecting clients to classes in the area
- *Nutrition apps*: for tracking calories and macros—just be careful with clients who might have eating disorder concerns

- *Water apps*: for tracking basic hydration—something many of us struggle with
- *Mindfulness apps*: for teaching mindfulness skills

Tip #8 · Integrating Teletherapy for Millennials

The idea of seeing therapy clients virtually can be highly polarizing for clinicians. Some rejoice at the idea of skipping their commute and staying in their cozy slippers to see clients, while others scoff at the idea and cannot imagine therapy is able to maintain its integrity when done across power lines. The reality is that the advent of telehealth is rapidly evolving. Not only are virtual practices offering much-needed services to rural populations, but busy professionals (millennials chief among them) also derive significant benefit from having one less place at which they need to be.

There are countless reasons to consider integrating teletherapy into your practice, even if only for a few hours per week. A handful of major benefits for clients include:

- *Low Barrier to Entry*: One of the biggest challenges facing prospective therapy clients is that initial appointment. For many clients, there is the anxiety of finding the therapy office, sitting in the waiting room, and anxiously counting down the time. But with teletherapy, it's almost always in the comfort of their home. What better way for clients to start therapy and open up than in their safe space?
- *Privacy*: The degree of privacy that in-person therapy offers certainly varies depending on the geographical location of a therapist's office and the diversity of clients that a therapist sees, but teletherapy ensures maximal privacy every time. Most therapists have experienced clients who are uncomfortable running into an old friend, boss, or colleague at the therapist's office. This never happens when therapy is done online.
- *Efficiency*: Time is perhaps our most precious resource, and having to commute to therapy appointments can be frustrating and stressful for clients already prone to anxiety. Unexpected traffic closures often lead clients to race into session, anxious about being late or missing any part of their therapy time. With teletherapy, this is far less of a concern.
- *Flexibility:* Relatedly, teletherapy allows for maximal flexibility for overworked and overcommitted clients. For clients with severe anxiety that is otherwise well-managed, the ability to schedule an emergency check-in can also be invaluable.
- *Safety:* Across much of the nation, severe winter weather can put a kink in plans. Clients have to debate whether to leave their homes in dangerous weather, worry about late cancellation fees, and consider which school districts are opened or closed. With teletherapy, the show can go on each time.

- ***Illness***: It is not uncommon for millennials with heavy workloads and many pressures to repeatedly succumb to illnesses. I have had clients with severe flus and viruses (often actively contagious) come into session, which puts me—and by extension my other clients—at risk. Further, illness often causes additional last-minute cancellations. The ability for clients to continue working with their therapist, especially when ill, can be highly impactful.

- ***Improved Timeliness:*** When sessions begin at the click of a button, timeliness improves. Because clients are almost always in reach of their devices, there are no concerns about getting stuck in a traffic jam, getting lost on the way to the office, or running low on gas.

- ***Access to Facilities, Food, Drink***: Most therapists have encountered ravenous clients eating and drinking while they are in session, in the waiting room, or walking out the door. Being able to satisfy a client's basic needs is certainly important. One of the benefits of teletherapy is access to any needs that may come up for a client, down to a bathroom with no line (without the risk of running into the therapist in the next stall over either).

- ***Access for Remote Clients***: It is not uncommon for clients who live in remote locations to report taking multiple buses or commuting for an hour to get to therapy. So much time and headache are saved when they can do therapy from home.

- ***Access for Clients with Disabilities:*** In many scenarios, clients who are bedridden, have chronic illness, or experience other concerns can benefit from online treatment options. For example, clients suffering from irritable bowel syndrome, Crohn's disease, or other conditions may experience shame or embarrassment at their need for leaving to use the facilities. In an online context, some of these concerns can be diminished considerably. Further, wheelchair accessibility can be a significant barrier with many populations as well. Ideally, more office buildings and clinics will become ADA-accessible, but the unfortunate reality is that in older locations and historic buildings, making these changes can take time and in other cases be impossible.

- ***Reduced Wait Times***: Although it is perhaps obvious, it is well-worth stating that teletherapy offers the benefit of near immediate access. Having worked in large clinics, I have observed insurance teams taking weeks to confirm benefits and process paperwork, amongst other bureaucratic hassles. For clients able to see private practitioners, access with teletherapy can be near immediate. With virtually all aspects of my practice being paperless and electronic, I can send paperwork to clients via a secure connection and have them fill it out and send it back to me within the day. Most often, I can accommodate clients within a week, if not 24 hours, depending on how quickly we can get things going. For clients who are in need to talk to someone urgently, or who have perhaps finally mustered up the courage to see someone, waiting weeks can lead to appointment cancellations or result in more dire situations.

Becoming Social Media Savvy

Tip #9 — Understanding the Big Four: Facebook, Instagram, Snapchat, and Twitter

Familiarizing yourself with the "Big Four" can go a long way in helping you to connect with your millennial client. Chances are that you already have some knowledge of, or even possess, an active social media account. Often to the frustration of many millennials, their boomer parents are plugging in and connecting eagerly with social media. Many boomers now have Facebook accounts and frequently "friend request" their children, nieces, and nephews. They may comment upon what they see, approve, and very often disapprove of. To say the least, social media makes the life of millennials complicated in many ways. In the event you may be newer to understanding these technologies, use the following chart for a quick primer on these popular social media platforms (Benson, 2019).

Facebook	Instagram	Twitter	Snapchat
2.23 billion monthly active users	1 billion monthly active users	326 million monthly active users	300 million monthly active users
Social media site (and mobile app) that allows sharing of links, photos, and videos, and intends to connect individuals to other people they know	Social sharing app focused on pictures and short videos	Microblogging site that limits posts to a 280-character limit	App that sends photos and videos that disappear upon viewing
1 million links shared every 20 minutes	95 million posts per day	Average of 6,000 tweets every second	10+ billion video views daily
25% of users are ages 25-34	Many brands heavily use hashtags and "influencers" to promote products and services	Over 69 million Twitter users in the U.S.	70% of users are female

 In-Session Tip:
Social media can be a large and ubiquitous trigger for many millennials. Opening the door to these discussions is a way to build rapport and engage with them on a deeper level. The world of social media can be a complex one fraught with embellishment, aggression, and insecurity on the part of those who post and receive these messages. Helping millennials acknowledge how much these technologies truly impact them on a day-to-day basis can prove fruitful.

In addition to the "Big Four," the world of social media is ever-growing. While you needn't worry about being an expert and avid user of any of these sites, it can help to stay abreast of the latest developments in additional social media technologies.

Pinterest

A site that is described as "all about discovery." This site is often deemed the inspiration for anything from nursery designs and party favor ideas to kitchen remodel designs. Pinterest is all about photos that can be a springboard for ideas and even dreams. Not unlike old-fashioned vision boards, individuals can create private or public boards to collect images of what they might like in a home, a vacation, or even certain fashions and style of dress.

YouTube

While many are familiar with YouTube, this platform has expanded significantly since its initial conception. Vloggers, or video bloggers, often have hundreds of thousands of followers based on their topic of interest. For example, many millennials might follow accounts dedicated to fitness, health, fashion, or any other number of domains. The concept of "YouTube famous" came about from musicians recording and posting videos of themselves on YouTube only to be discovered and backed by major recording artists. Justin Bieber, one of the world's best-selling music artists, is one such example. As a result, many (but not all!) YouTubers have discovery and fame in mind when posting videos of themselves and creating content. It is not uncommon (albeit bizarre) for mini-celebrities to emerge from YouTube, which can also explain why some exhibit narcissistic behaviors and tendencies in their videos.

LinkedIn

Commonly thought of as a work or professional form of social media, LinkedIn has also expanded its reach in efforts to keep up with, and add functionality similar to, other social media sites. The original purpose of LinkedIn was to connect professionals to other individuals within their network and with others they may know or want to collaborate with. Over time, though, LinkedIn revised its homepage to feature a "feed" like the "Big Four" social media platforms. Photos, videos, and comments can now be posted, which allows for more interaction between users.

Tip #11 | Prepare for New Emerging Technologies

Developing familiarity with and a working knowledge of social media can be intimidating to say the least. Few things can make a therapist feel "old" and "out of touch" as much as hearing about the latest trend, terminology, or social media platform to emerge without a clue as to what they mean. The good news is that no one knows *all* of the existing technology, including millennial and younger generations. The main idea is to remain open and interested in learning more.

Don't fear asking your millennial client to open up an app and show you how it works or to discuss what they find to be particularly interesting or even triggering. I've had clients share the most obscure apps that very few people use. Showing an interest, and then later doing my own homework, has helped significantly in being able to share the same language with my clients.

Finally, you might just get into the habit of dropping into computer stores from time to time to play with the latest gadgets. You might learn about new apps and even be amazed at how much has been digitized and can lead to a more streamlined experience. For example, watches can now store music, audible books, and podcasts that you can play in wireless earbuds while checking the weather and still getting messages from your kids—if you choose to enable such options. No need to go overboard, but you get the idea.

Tech Tip:

One confounding aspect of all these forms of technologies (with the possible exception of YouTube) is that they all feature messaging capabilities. So you may hear terms such as "DM me" referring to a direct message on Instagram. Or, a client might use Facebook messenger exclusively instead of regular text message (which basically achieves the same thing a text would). The medium often doesn't matter—it is important instead to focus on the message itself.

A second detail to be aware of is that these technologies sometimes report when a message is opened or viewed. This can be the cause of much angst among millennials as they now know someone opened their message and intentionally did not reply back. Be prepared for such discussions as you might otherwise be confused how a client could be certain that someone was ignoring them on social media.

Social Media Tip:

A final tip to be aware of: In these times of technologies, social media gets many people into deep trouble. All it takes is for someone to take a screenshot of a "drunk text" (a message sent when the individual was inebriated), or to post an inappropriate Instagram photo that is immediately taken down, in order for them to experience much distress (and in extreme scenarios, for them to be fired from a job or broken up with). Digital history can lead to much social ostracization and shame, so it is highly educational to have frank conversations with your millennial client about what is appropriate and inappropriate to share on social media. It is not uncommon for bloggers and influencers to cross boundaries so frequently that individuals may not realize the consequences of mimicking these behaviors.

Part 2

problem solving

speedy solutions for millennials

Solution-Focused Therapy

Given that many millennials have limited time and financial resources to devote to therapy, solution-focused therapy (SFT) can yield the biggest therapeutic improvements in the shortest amount of time. Often utilized in mental health clinics and college counseling centers to manage client crises, the beauty of SFT lies in its simplicity. While it is certainly not the same thing as advice-giving, it does involve identifying a handful of small solutions to keep concerns at bay. For an anxious millennial client, these solutions may range from turning their devices off at night and creating better work boundaries, to using exercise to burn off anxious energy. When clients are struggling, there are usually a few immediate tweaks they can make to improve their overall mood and functioning. Many times, a client simply needs permission to sleep more, go to that yoga class, say no to excessive social functions, or cut down on caffeine.

To help clients problem-solve through their concerns, SFT is known for making use of the "miracle question" technique—the idea of asking a client if a miracle happened and their problem went away, what life would look like. Oftentimes, this question helps clients realize that a miracle is usually not warranted to solve their problem. For example, if a client is experiencing significant difficulties in philosophy class, then the solution may be to drop the class and take it next semester with a new professor. Or if their concern is about not getting a much-wanted job promotion, then they can apply for jobs elsewhere or talk directly to their boss. You don't need a miracle to solve these problems.

One of the best way to build the therapeutic relationship in the context of SFT is to compliment clients for their strengths. For example, you can compliment clients for identifying solutions, having self-awareness, and seeking help in the first place. You can even compliment their ability to recognize when they don't know something and to express vulnerability. Since SFT is brief by nature (often about five sessions total), building rapport through the use of complimenting techniques can help propel the relationship forward and allow depth of exploration to develop more rapidly.

Throughout this section, you will find tools and handouts most relevant to the practice of SFT. These include resources on sleep, diet, exercise, time management, procrastination, perfectionism, and self-care. As you work on setting up these building blocks of well-being, keep the following key principles in mind (de Shazer & Berg, 1995):

- If it isn't broken, don't fix it.
- Once you know what works, do more of it.
- If it's not working, do something differently.

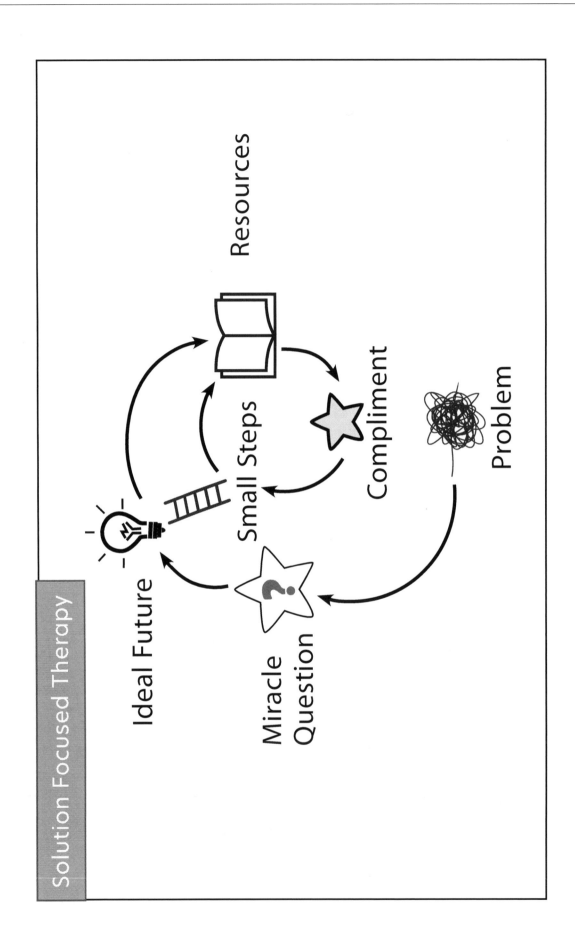

Tool #1 | Sleep Hygiene Hints

THERAPIST OVERVIEW

Modern millennials are unfortunately all too familiar with chronic fatigue and exhaustion. After all, there is a reason they have been dubbed the "Burnout Generation" (Petersen, 2019). From a young age, many millennials have become accustomed to functioning with far less sleep than the body needs to function properly. Because millennials have so many constraints on their time and are engaged in endless multitasking, by the time they have a moment to slow down, it might be past midnight. Tired and wanting to wind down, they may turn to technology, which instead of soothing their weary mind, only serves to further activate it. They might intend to check their social media feed for ten minutes only to see an hour slip by. Or, an endless texting thread with friends can go on for hours. Whether due to technology (and the blue light that stimulates their brains), or the sheer busyness of life, millennials are in dire need of more sleep.

Although sleep is highly elusive for anxious millennial minds, the idea of setting aside more time and creating a routine may initially be met with resistance, as there is always one more thing for millennials to do. Encourage clients to choose one area where they can improve their sleep each week to slowly add on elements of good sleep hygiene. Also, don't be shy about using your tech-knowledge to suggest that they use the "night shift" settings on their devices to limit the amount of blue light emitted prior to sleep onset. Walking them through an example of what good sleep hygiene looks like can be helpful. I often start by discussing dimming lights two hours prior to bed, cleaning up dishes, and turning off the computer, and then shift to discussing how one might take a bath, meditate, or journal. Creating a narrative that they can then apply to their own life and circumstances is helpful and instructive.

Tech Tip:

Many millennials love using technology to track things, including sleep, but this can be a double-edged sword: While data can be useful, it can also keep them connected all through the night. Have a conversation with your client about what is most practical for their particular concern. I have had clients sometimes use sleep tracking apps very intentionally and mindfully—and they truly use the app (or calming sleep meditation) to sleep soundly and well, and not as an excuse to check their social media feed one last time.

Sleep Hygiene Hints

Duration: 10-15 minutes	**Frequency:** As Needed	**Level of Difficulty:** Easy

Instructions: Here are some of the components related to good sleep hygiene. Put a checkmark next the ones you already do, and put an X next to the ones you need to work on integrating into your nighttime routine. See if you can challenge yourself over the next week to maintain your healthy habits and incorporate one or two new ideas each night.

_____ Avoid caffeinated foods and beverages (chocolate counts!) up to four to six hours prior to sleep. If you are sensitive to excess sugars, also refrain from eating sugar several hours prior to sleep.

_____ Avoid any and all alcoholic beverages before nighttime. While many enjoy a nightcap or glass of wine to unwind, alcohol can negatively impact overall sleep quality.

_____ Reserve your bed for sleep-related activities only. Do not do paperwork, check emails, or even read for extensive periods of time in your bed.

_____ Turn off all electronic devices or anything with a screen two hours prior to bed.

_____ Consider activating any features on your phone that keep it from emitting blue light at night. On some phones this is called the "night shift" feature, and it allows you to set a time when the phone goes into this mode. This can also serve as a reminder of when you need to put away electronic devices.

_____ Find a comfortable temperature for sleep so you are not too hot or cold to fall asleep. The ideal temperature for many is between 65 and 72 degrees.

_____ Start preparing your body for sleep by slowly dimming the lights around you one to two hours prior to sleep. This helps signal to the body to start winding down for the evening.

_____ Consider taking a warm bath or shower to relax the muscles and wash away the day one hour prior to sleep.

_____ If reading before bed is relaxing to you, consider reading for 10-15 minutes while in bed. If the material is too activating, it can wake up the mind. You don't want to spend too much time in bed doing non sleep-related activities, though, so be sure to keep an eye on the clock.

_____ Consider a meditation, short prayer, or gentle stretches before bed. While you ideally don't want to sleep with a phone in your bedroom, there are some excellent meditation apps available that utilize yoga nidra (a type of sleep-related meditation) that can relax you prior to sleep.

_____ Do not go to bed hungry or overly full. Both scenarios can negatively impact sleep. There is some research indicating that the calcium and magnesium in dairy milk or yogurt can assist with sleep. However, if you abstain from dairy, consider a light snack if you're hungry, and do not eat a large meal immediately prior to sleep.

_____ Consider relaxing herbal teas prior to bed. Many stores sell chamomile or lavender teas that can help to relax you. Be sure to check with a doctor if you find a sleep concoction tea in order to make sure it is safe to ingest.

_____ Avoid relying on over-the-counter medications or melatonin for sleep. Even though you do not need a prescription for these medications, this does not make them completely safe. Some can be habit-forming or addictive, so saving these medications for use on an "emergency basis" is a much safer bet.

_____ Try to have as much of a regular routine as possible so your body slowly becomes attuned to when it is time for sleep.

Tool #2 | Assessing and Improving Diet

THERAPIST OVERVIEW

Relative to other generations, millennials are fairly diet-conscious, in a healthy and body-positive way. The realities of the fast food and convenience food eras have set in, and millennials are ever more aware of how critical a healthy diet is. While some might say their trends are taken to an extreme, at the end of the day, millennials are driven toward diets for reasons related to health, longevity, and wellness.

However, it can also be daunting for millennials to navigate the plethora of available dietary and lifestyle choices. From the popularity of vegan to ketogenic diets, there are extremes to say the least. Choosing to eat only plants or only fats are quite disparate sides of the continuum, and many millennials can get caught up in one trend or the other. Social media is particularly powerful in this domain, as influencers and food bloggers capture how their particular dietary choices lead to their sculpted physiques and flat abs. These same influencers are often compensated by companies who incidentally give them free, unlimited access to collagen supplements, protein shakes, and coffee mixes, hence blurring the line between true health food breakthroughs and gimmicks.

Millennials' tendency to experiment with diet extremes does not need be a downfall and in many ways can be a strength. Millennials are highly open-minded when it comes to trying out various dietary changes to achieve a healthier lifestyle. The goal for therapists is to help clients determine what they see as healthy for their own body types without worrying about dieting, restricting foods, or copying what the latest fad diet may be.

Clients can start to take note of what they consume during a typical day on the following worksheet. By turning their attention and awareness toward the importance of a healthy diet, clients can easily come to see where they might be lacking in greens, proteins, or fiber, and how this may be impacting their physical (and emotional) health. The goal is to avoid any sort of calorie counting or judgment but to just take note. For clients who struggle with eating disorders, caution must be taken with any type of food tracking activity, so it's wise to assess what level of food intake they feel comfortable tracking and sharing. When feasible, collaborating with a nutritionist is helpful in ensuring a client's dietary choices support healthy functioning. Many workplaces now offer nutritional counseling as a part of their benefit packages, and many colleges employ nutritionists on their medical staff. Encouraging clients to connect with these professionals can help support your work at large.

Terminology Tip:

The term "hangry" certainly emerged during the millennial era, which describes the irritability or anger some individuals experience as a result of hunger. A recognition of the body's state when pushed to the extremes of constantly skipping or delaying meals, getting hangry is a concept far too many millennials complain of. Beyond being regarded as an annoyance, keeping irritation at bay is important for numerous reasons. When the instigator is something as simple as staying well-fed, there is no reason for millennials to snap at their partners and co-workers because they are in actuality starving.

Tech Tip:

While apps such as MyFitnessPal® are highly popular and can be useful for tracking macros and calories, it is helpful to exercise some caution when using these apps. That being said, for clients who struggle with undereating, or who have a healthy approach to weight loss, such apps can help them stay on track and make sure they are eating enough and meeting all of their nutritional needs.

Social Media Tip:

YouTube, Instagram, and Snapchat stories can incidentally be useful for some clients, assuming they follow food bloggers who advocate for nutrient-dense foods that are easy to prepare and realistic for clients to integrate into their diets. The idea of "meal prepping" certain foods ahead of time, such as overnight oats and mason jar salads, has gained increasing popularity among millennials as they allow for ease, speed, and nutrition. Encouraging clients to devote some energy to healthy meal planning can benefit countless other areas of their lives.

Assessing and Improving Diet

Duration: 15-20 minutes	**Frequency:** Daily	**Level of Difficulty:** Moderate

Instructions: Over the next week, take some time to notice what you are eating in a day. The goal is not to count calories. Instead, you are looking to make sure you are eating enough and that the quality of foods is high as well. If you are prone to mindless eating, pay attention to serving sizes. Be as honest as you can. While you may be tempted to highlight the best in your eating, you have to be completely transparent in order to improve or sustain healthy eating patterns. Use the chart on the next page to track your food intake. After you have recorded your food consumption for one week, answer the following reflection questions.

After tracking your food consumption for the last week, what are your major observations?

_____

_____

_____

What behaviors might you need to change?

_____

_____

_____

How can you improve your overall diet?

_____

_____

_____

client worksheet

Food Log

	Monday	Tuesday	Wednesday	Thursday	Friday	Saturday	Sunday
Breakfast							
Midmorning Snack							
Lunch							
Afternoon Snack							
Dinner							
Post-Dinner Snack							
Number of Carbohydrate Servings							
Number of Protein Servings							
Number of Fat Servings							

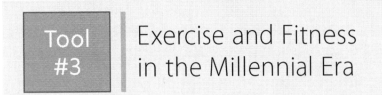

Tool #3

Exercise and Fitness in the Millennial Era

THERAPIST OVERVIEW

With so much already on millennials' plates, the idea of carving out even more time for exercise can be challenging. However, with an increase in sedentary lifestyles, as well as the rise of telecommuting jobs that don't even require leaving the house, millennials are spending much of their lives sitting. A couple of decades ago, the computer may have been the only screen that workers hunched over, but the ubiquity of cell phones has made millennials connected to their jobs around the clock. Therefore, helping them integrate fitness into their routines is more important than ever before. Some millennials swing back and forth between extremes when it comes to exercise, such as taking demanding "bootcamp" style classes only to burnout and do no exercise months later. For this reason, finding a sustainable long-term and dynamic exercise plan is key. Not only can regular exercise improve sleep and anxiety, but it can help counteract the many negative effects of screen time.

Therapists don't need be fitness coaches or experts to help clients integrate physical activity into their lives. If you want to help your client get more active, the best course of action is usually to find out what type of exercise or fitness they enjoyed in the past. Upon assessment, you might be surprised to learn a client was an avid swimmer back in middle school, or that they once did gymnastics but quit after an injury. Others simply enjoy taking the dog for a walk. Starting small is key, as many millennials are eager to jump the gun and then wind up disappointed when they realize their cardiovascular system or muscles are not as conditioned for exercise as they used to be.

Naturopathic expert Dr. John Douillard discusses the importance of matching exercise with body type in order to determine the best type of physical activity for each person. He provides guidance for assessing body types (or body temperaments), as well as different types of sports well-suited to these types. These three body types are Spring, Summer, and Winter. Those with a Spring temperament are described as having a solid, heavy physical build predisposed to strength and endurance. They have a tranquil personality and are slow to irritability or excitement. Summer types have a more moderate build and are prone to irritability and anger. Winter types are of lighter, thinner builds who are prone to anxiety. And while some individuals may purely represent one body type, it is possible for combined types to also exist.

Given the inherent differences in body types, the same expectations cannot be set for athletic performance across all bodies. Clients who are intrinsically gifted at lifting weights may not be light enough on their feet to be an accomplished dancer. While this is certainly not to discourage individuals from trying out activities not ideally suited to their bodies, this does help build confidence in pursuing sports and activities at which one would naturally be stronger. When clients feel confident and adept, they are more likely to pursue and keep up these forms of exercise over the long haul.

The following handout describes different types of physical activities that are best-suited for each body type. (For additional information on combined types and a more precise assessment, refer clients to conduct their own exploration of these concepts on Dr. Douillard's website or in his book, *Body, Mind, and Sport* (2001), which is listed in the Recommended Readings section.)

Terminology Tip:

Never before in history have hashtags such as #fitnessgoals been front and center for a generation. While millennials' awareness regarding the importance of exercise is a major strength for a generation that grew up during the obesity and diabetes epidemic, as with many endeavors, millennials can also get carried away. Countless images of sculpted bodies, or of people lifting and squatting, have normalized intensive exercise and provided millennials with specific ideas about what being "healthy" looks like. Some millennials are driven by an inner fire and competitiveness to keep up with these trends, while others are overwhelmed and cycle through periods of intensive activity followed by complete inactivity. Restoring a sense of balance and engaging in healthy (even low-impact) activity can be a major adjunct to therapy treatment.

Social Media Tip:

The incessant social media and cultural demands on physique have led some millennials experiencing depressive and anxious symptoms to avoid the gym and exercise altogether due to shame related to body image and comparisons with peers. Too many times, the endorphin rush that can help motivate clients toward healthy change is never experienced because they have a chronic avoidance of and even aversion to exercise. Consider encouraging clients to "follow" a healthy fitness role model on social media. Maybe it is a mom getting back in shape after pregnancy (in a healthy manner!) or a busy professional sharing how he makes time for fitness throughout the workday.

Tech Tip:

Many experts warn against the use of electronic devices during exercise, as a distracted mind can miss important cues regarding pain and the need to back off from a certain level of exertion. That said, many millennials are also used to multitasking and listening to podcasts while performing many ordinary tasks. Assess and use your best judgment as to what might work for your client. Some millennials who are very resistant to any form of movement might be motivated by watching Netflix while walking a mile or two on the treadmill. Others who are already drowning in excessive tech usage would benefit from taking a step back during exercise and treating this time as a tech-free retreat of sorts.

Exercise and Fitness in the Millennial Era

Duration: 15-20 minutes	**Frequency:** As Needed	**Level of Difficulty:** Moderate

Instructions: Finding time for fitness is one of the greatest keys to unlocking your optimal well-being. In our ever-busy life, though, one of the first things that many people cut out is their exercise routine. Maybe getting dressed and going to the gym is too cumbersome, as it turns into a two-hour ordeal that leaves you coming home famished. Or, perhaps those yoga classes feel too slow and boring. Finding what fits your unique needs is a major part of finding an exercise regimen that works for you and that you can stick to. Have a number of key activities you cycle through if you are prone to getting bored or uninspired by the same old activities.

In the following chart, you can find various activities that are best-suited to one of three different body types, as described by Dr. John Douillard, a leading expert in the field of health, wellness, and sports medicine.

Identify your body type using the descriptors in Step 1, and then put a checkmark by the activities you are most interested in integrating into your weekly routine in Step 2. You might even circle what you already do, and check what you are interested in trying out or adding in.

Step 1: Identify Your Body Type

Winter	Spring	Summer
Build: Lighter, thinner	**Build:** Solid, heavy build; Have strength and endurance	**Build:** Moderate
Temperament: Prone to anxiety		**Temperament:** Prone to irritability and anger
	Temperament: Tranquil, slow to irritability or excitement	
Sleep: Light sleepers		**Sleep:** Sound, medium sleepers
	Sleep: Long, heavy sleepers	
Digestion: Irregular hunger cues and a tendency toward digestive issues		**Digestion:** Cannot skip meals due to their tendency to feel extreme hunger
	Digestion: Have slower digestion without sharp hunger cues	

Step 2: Identify Fitness Activities to Complement Your Body Type

Winter Body Types	Spring Body Types	Summer Body Types
Suited to activities that are slow and calming, and that help with rejuvenation instead of exhaustion, such as:	Suited to activities that are stimulating and intense, which helps motivate those with a slower inclination toward movement, such as:	Suited to activities that balance heat and competitiveness, and that promote enjoyment instead of competition, such as:
___ Low-impact aerobics	___ Aerobics	___ Hockey
___ Dance	___ Basketball	___ Surfing
___ Ice skating	___ Soccer	___ Wind surfing
___ Kayaking	___ Swimming	___ Water skiing
___ Yoga	___ Tennis	___ Football
___ Bowling	___ Shotput	___ Mountain biking
___ Badminton	___ Javelin	___ Diving
___ Ballet	___ Bodybuilding	___ Downhill skiing
___ Bicycle touring	___ Fencing	___ Cross-country skiing
___ Golf	___ Cross-country running	___ Golf
___ Doubles tennis	___ Cross-country skiing	___ Ice skating
___ Hiking	___ Volleyball	___ Yoga
___ Walking	___ Lacrosse	___ Sailing
___ Sailing	___ Rock climbing	___ Martial arts
___ Swimming	___ Fencing	___ Kayaking/rowing
___ Easy rowing/canoeing	___ Rowing	___ Racquet sports
___ Horseback riding	___ Racquetball	___ Basketball and other team sports
___ Martial arts	___ Handball	
___ Ping pong	___ In-line skating	
___ Weight training	___ Cycling	
___ Baseball	___ Gymnastics	

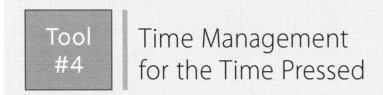

Tool #4 | Time Management for the Time Pressed

THERAPIST OVERVIEW

Many millennials struggle with overcommitment and chronic multitasking. Asking millennials to take a step back to assess what is truly urgent and important is a lifelong skill they can use to better manage their time. With an incessant stream of emails coming in from bosses, or Snapchats from friends and other various inputs, practicing time management skills can help to significantly ease anxiety.

Clients can learn to better manage their time by creating a list of all the outstanding items on their to-do list and then simply marking them as urgent or not urgent, and important or not important. This helps simplify what the demands on their time are. You might even walk your client through their tasks from morning until night to make sure they cover everything that takes up their time. This will prevent them from only focusing on factors related to work and help them see how their time might be spent more efficiently when they get home, or when they get up first thing in the morning.

After getting into the habit of listing their time commitments and assessing their importance and urgency, encourage clients to find a time management system that works for them. Many therapy clients insist their phone calendar is best, while others use Google calendar®. While going paperless is commendable and can streamline various calendar systems, for very busy or even disorganized clients, starting with a paper planner can help them visualize how their time is spent. Further, paper planners can add an element of tangibility as clients manually highlight and cross items off their to-do list. They can also add Post-it® notes, clip in business cards, or add other important papers as needed.

The goal is certainly not for clients to end up with a hefty paper planner that is not easily portable, but there are a number of solid planners available with tools aimed at helping individuals set work and personal goals, as well as track and manage mood. You want to help clients get organized, as this sets them up for success in reaching their goals. At the same time, the planning and time management process should be enjoyable, positive, and fun. So it's important clients spend a good amount of time finding what works best for them.

Finally, it's worth encouraging clients to re-assess their goals and tasks on a monthly basis to allow a fresh perspective and start. Clients can become discouraged when they do not feel they are making progress or are going in circles, so it is a powerful practice to treat each month as a fresh start to list goals, plans, and intentions. Many millennials are already familiar with the idea of setting monthly intentions, which can include small goals (drink more water) and big goals (start writing that novel). Having a planner that can be used almost as a journal can facilitate long-term as well as short-term goals.

Time Management
for the Time Pressed

Duration: 10-30 minutes	Frequency: Weekly	Level of Difficulty: Moderate

Instructions: Developed by author and businessman Stephen Covey (2013), a "time management matrix" can help you manage all your competing demands once and for all. The following matrix shows four quadrants indicating the importance versus urgency of an item. Learning to prioritize what is truly urgent, and what can be dealt with later, can ease your anxiety significantly.

Some sample entries are provided, followed by a blank copy where you can list your most pressing items and the tasks that take away your attention. Be sure to pay special attention to tasks that fall in the fourth quadrant ("not important" and "not urgent"), as you might use these tasks to procrastinate from work that falls in the more urgent and important spaces.

	Urgent	Not Urgent
Important	Prepare financial analysis for boss that is due tomorrow.	Pay monthly bills on time, update passport, book dentist appointment.
Not Important	Interruptions, emails, phone calls, text messages.	Watching television, web surfing, browsing social media.

Time Management

	Urgent	Not Urgent
Important		
Not Important		

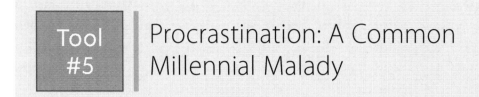

Tool #5 | Procrastination: A Common Millennial Malady

THERAPIST OVERVIEW

Procrastination is a common concern among many younger demographics. Whether it is a high school student who puts off completing that paper until the last minute only to have a parent call in an absence for them, or a college student begging a professor for an extension, examples of procrastination abound. While procrastination is definitely an affliction among wiser and more mature populations as well, for millennials who are only beginning to make their mark on the professional world, remnants of their college approach to life can constantly resurface, setting them behind in their work and chipping away at their sense of self-efficacy. While a junior law associate might be able to get away with responding to emails instead of getting work done on a major case, when it comes time for promotions and other work perks, timeliness and quality work completion are almost always rewarded.

Helping clients identify the core reason for their procrastination is a highly valuable but exceedingly challenging task. While low-grade procrastinators may put off a single task or a series of tasks with little major impact to their daily lives, chronic procrastinators may dread every day and live with enormous amounts of guilt, shame, and distress. In order to problem-solve chronic procrastination, clients can follow a series of easily identifiable steps, which involve identifying a cause for the procrastination, working backwards to prevent triggers, optimizing the work environment, and enlisting the help of "accountability buddies." However, the work of the therapist is more challenging. Ultimately, it involves much processing to determine the root cause of these behaviors and what the emotional blockages may be. Is the client suffering from shame? Is their intense need for perfection preventing them from getting started on a project due to the desire to make things just right? As many therapists know, perfectionism is the close cousin of procrastination, and these two often (but not necessarily always) go hand in hand.

An assessment of emotional factors can also be informative in the treatment process. For example, intense anxiety can be paralyzing to a client and thus impact their tendency toward procrastination. Likewise, depression can naturally diminish motivation and drive due to the low energy and fatigue that can accompany this condition. As a general rule, it is often helpful to assess for procrastination and perfectionism when clients present with any number of emotional distress concerns.

Tech Tip:

While procrastination is a concern that has impacted a host of generations, the advent of digital technologies has certainly impacted and exacerbated procrastination among millennials in particular. When bosses now have the ability to text their employees, many millennials are juggling multiple technologies simply to do their jobs. Unfortunately, this can also be the very same medium that family, friends, and partners may use to contact them. For example, it is very easy for millennials to quickly get sidetracked when they go to respond to a work email and a sudden bridal shower invitation pops up—which then leads them to RSVP and spend time buying a gift from the registry before the preferred items are already taken. Therefore, make sure to have a discussion with clients regarding technology as a distraction and accomplice to procrastination.

Millennial Vignette:

I will never forget the millennial client who came to me with the explicit presenting concern of procrastination. Whereas many clients usually present for other reasons—and procrastination is later discovered as a culprit in their mood and work progress—this particular client was well aware of his Achilles' heel. Even more promising was that I was the third or fourth therapist he was seeing for this issue. He had researched it, knew what he needed to do, came regularly to therapy, but just couldn't force himself to sit down and work on the task at hand. To be honest, therapy often went in circles. We processed his guilt and discussed strategies for better time management, including the reinforcement of schedules, but nothing worked. Even work on self-compassion and patience was of little help. In the end, I don't know that I helped him at all, which is always sobering as a therapist, as we pride ourselves on being helpers and healers. But what I learned most was how incredibly challenging it can be to aid clients in overcoming chronic procrastination.

Procrastination: A Common Millennial Malady

| **Duration:** 10-15 minutes | **Frequency:** As Needed | **Level of Difficulty:** Moderate |

Instructions: Procrastination is a common millennial malady, but fortunately there are a number of ways you can overcome it. In this three-part activity, you will be challenged to identify your common procrastination pitfalls, write and reflect, and then come up with a solid plan to help make your life procrastination-proof.

First, read the statements below and check off your most common procrastination pitfalls:

☐ **Perfectionism.** For many, a desire to do things when fully rested and energized, or when inspiration hits, can be a major cause of procrastination. They need to be in the perfect frame of mind, but even if this happens, they may feel the work itself is never done or good enough.

☐ **Task Ambiguity.** It is common to be assigned a task, even be excited about it, but realize you don't fully possess the skills or knowledge to complete it. For example, maybe you need to produce a pamphlet, book, or other publication. Even if you know the content (or know where to search for it), it may not be until you get a template or sample that you understand how to do the task and feel comfortable approaching it.

☐ **Over-Dramatizing a Task.** We all know that person: They bring their laptop to their one and only vacation, are on a conference call during a pedicure, and have their earpiece in at the gym. The semblance of being so busy or so important can actually impact procrastination. That's because you dramatize or make a task out to be much bigger than it is. In turn, you keep putting it off and tell others you can't go out as you have "that big project" to complete—but you never actually work on it.

☐ **Underestimating a Task.** You finally sit down to complete a task and are overwhelmed that it's actually far more time-consuming than you may have thought. Perhaps you did not budget enough time and panic sets in. This leads you to completely avoid the task altogether.

☐ **Technology Distractions.** Social media, texts, emails, Netflix, you name it. You intend to browse through your phone for ten minutes, and that quickly turns into hours. You keep putting off the dread of the task for the momentary pleasure (and guilt) of indulging in technology.

☐ **Boring, Uninteresting, or Uninspiring Tasks**. Many times, the reason for procrastination is quite obvious and self-evident: The task is of little to no inherent interest and feels like busy work. It can seem like you're hardly making an impact when you're assigned tasks not related to your skillset or job description. In turn, you may feel underappreciated at work or may even be considering a job change.

☐ **Fear of Failure**. Oftentimes, a fear of not performing well prevents people from attempting a task at all. Maybe a promotion is riding on a project, or you were hired as the new young hotshot and are scared you'll disappoint everyone who went out on a limb to hire you.

Now that you have read through and checked off some of the most common sources of procrastination, spend some time reflecting on your answers and record any additional thoughts, observations, or insights regarding your procrastination:

_____

_____

_____

Now, get ready to make some changes! While there are hundreds of books written on the topic, there are a number of key factors that can significantly help with procrastination. While you are ideally working through this workbook with a therapist, getting support is key to unlocking the particular combination of factors that could be impacting you. For some people, procrastination is related to perfectionism, while for others it's related to boredom, so there is definitely no one-size-fits-all approach. The steps listed here are just some factors to consider in tackling your unique brand of procrastination.

Step 1: Start with Compassion

Be kind to yourself! The essentials are simple: By watching your self-talk and being kind and patient with yourself, you set yourself up for success. If you are already feeling stressed or upset about your procrastination, a negative frame of mind only makes things worse. So start with a positive and healthy mindset and attitude.

Step 2: Get Support

Whether a therapist, best friend, co-worker, or partner, enlisting others to help us can make a major difference. Maybe you've been wanting to go to the gym and never quite make it—get a workout buddy. If a work project has been a bear, get an empathic co-worker to coach you on, and you can help keep them accountable too.

Step 3: Optimize Your Environment

Buy that multicolored keyboard cover or crazy mouse pad. Turn on the ocean waves track you have in your music files, and light that candle already. Do whatever it takes to get into your work-mode. In fact, it can be very Pavlovian. Whether or not you are in the mood, if you always brew the same type of tea, put on the same tunes, or do any number of ritualistic things, it can help convince you to get to work.

Step 4: Go Tech-Free

Hands down, one of the most common procrastination pitfalls is technology. You went online to email your boss and remembered your favorite store was running a limited sale, so now you're online shopping. Or, you hop on Insta to check how a work-related post is doing, and then you end up scrolling through your personal account and going down a rabbit hole of endless articles, pages, and stories. Cut the tech, cold turkey. If you have a deadline coming up, *do not* go on the Internet. Instead, put your phone on airplane mode, silence all alerts, and do whatever you need to do for a several hour block of time until you complete the task. Then, have at it. In fact, there are productivity apps that will force you to go off certain social media sites and technologies if you can't do it yourself.

Step 5: Maximize Time Management Skills

Maybe you are an organizational master, or perhaps it's one of your worst skills. If procrastination is an issue for you, then you must learn to manage your time. Maybe you start using a planner or calendar to plan out your week, or you program your phone to send you alerts when you need to switch tasks and move onto something else. Technology can be your friend in the right doses and can be used to help keep you on track. In an ideal world, a paper calendar can help you see an overview of the month and quarter ahead so you are never scrambling at the last minute to get things done or figure out when to do certain tasks. Organization can even help you build in a buffer for those days when you practice kindness and allow yourself a tiny bit of a detour from your task.

Step 6: Healthy Body, Healthy Mind

It can be tough to get work done when you are hungry, thirsty, or—even worse—under the influence. Whether it is a hangover from the night before, or you have been sitting for hours on end without getting up to stretch or exercise, taking care of your body is a key factor in helping your productivity. How many times have you been about to exercise or start a task when you realize your stomach is rumbling? Making sure to prioritize your basic needs can go a long way in fending off procrastination.

Step 7: Take Breaks

By the time some people get to working, they start to take on a somewhat obsessive stance and don't want to stop until the task is done. They are fueled by high doses of caffeine (bottomless cups of coffee or sodas), junk food, and whatever is fast and convenient so they don't have to break the "zone" they worked so hard to finally get to. While bursts of productivity are amazing and to be commended, martyrdom is certainly not a prerequisite for major accomplishments. So make it a habit to build in rest breaks, whether it's taking a few minutes to stand and stretch or even do some yoga.

Step 8: Reward Yourself

Many millennials survive a task only to move onto the next mountain before them. They don't take time to savor their successes or congratulate themselves for hard work. Or, if they do, it can involve unhealthy amounts of alcohol, junk food, and other indulgences that don't nourish their bodies. The next time you successfully complete a major task, consider planning a healthy and meaningful reward you can give yourself to celebrate. Can't think of one? Consider asking a therapist, friend, or partner who knows you well. They are often more than happy to help you come up with a joyful and healthy celebration.

Now that you have learned about ways to help with procrastination, write your personalized plan to help you overcome this common concern:

_____

_____

_____

_____

_____

_____

Tool #6 | Perfectionism Primer

THERAPIST OVERVIEW

Millennials put an incredible amount of pressure on themselves when it comes to the pursuit of perfection. Especially as a generation who came of age during the Great Recession, competition was intense for limited slots, whether it was internships or jobs. While only a decade ago law students could rely on handsome compensation for summer clerkships, those days are long gone. For millennials, simply getting a slot was a hard-earned task, and they were willing to do it for free. As someone who worked as a fellow at a health center without any health insurance benefits, I quickly came to see this reality as well. Even the most well-funded institutions make trainees work under the national poverty line with no benefits. When resources are so limited, it's easy to see how every single email, interaction in the hallway, or project feedback can be overanalyzed by even the least perfectionistic individuals among us. But for millennials who grew up fighting the "snowflake" stereotype—and who seek to live up to the standards of often demanding boomer parents—perfectionism has taken on a whole new meaning.

Therapy addressing perfectionism can take many shapes and forms. Whether it is the pursuit of aesthetic, professional, or social perfection, a common experience among millennials is intense pressure, self-criticism, doubt, and a desire to please (others or themselves). Discovering the root of these core beliefs can be helpful to the therapeutic work. Perhaps individuals were given the implicit message by their parents that to be perfect is to be loved completely. Or, as a result of peer rejection, they internalized a message that becoming perfect would result in acceptance. When clients experience this intense need to be perfect and fear failure if perfection is not attained, procrastination often ensues. In the activity that follows, clients will be encouraged to start thinking about the ways in which perfectionism may manifest in their lives.

Millennial Vignette:
In addition to discovering some of the roots of perfectionistic thinking, therapy can be an incredible place to practice these skills. For example, I once worked with a millennial graduate student studying architecture. Her program was highly competitive and deeply rooted in seeking perfection. Classmates would walk around and offer criticism and points of improvement, and my anxious client found herself in the studio well past midnight trying to perfect her work. Her perfectionism also manifested as an intense anxiety about time and being late. She would often attempt to come to therapy far in advance and felt intense guilt if she was in the lobby only minutes prior. I challenged her to repeatedly attempt to come to therapy late. For those who are always running late, this experiment may sound silly, but for those who have similar anxieties, the irrational fear is very readily experienced and a familiar one indeed. It can be an incredibly powerful practice to teach a client that being less than perfect is very much acceptable and that they will be fully loved and accepted regardless of their perfection. My client was able to learn from a very simple experiment that I was never mad at her, was always complimentary, and was deeply interested in listening to her experiences regardless of imperfection.

Perfectionism Primer

Duration: 1-5 minutes	**Frequency:** As Needed	**Level of Difficulty:** Moderate

Instructions: Perfectionism can mean different things to people. For some, it involves concern over mistakes, doubts about actions, personal standards, and the need to be organized. For others, it is related to parental expectations and criticism. Some of the most common factors involved in perfectionism are listed here (Stairs et. al, 2012). See if you recognize any of them in your own life.

☐ **Order:** You need everything in your environment to be neat, tidy, and clean. Everything must be in its place.

☐ **Details and Checking:** You have a tendency to be overly thorough in your work, focusing excessively on the details and checking and re-checking your work to ensure you haven't made any mistakes.

☐ **Perfectionism Toward Others:** You expect everyone to perform to your high standards and get frustrated or annoyed when people inevitably fail to live up to your expectations.

☐ **High Standards:** You set a high bar for yourself and push yourself to attain these standards, even if these standards are unreasonable.

☐ **Black-and-White Thinking:** You believe everything is either a success or complete failure. If something cannot be done perfectly, it is not worth trying at all.

☐ **Perceived Pressure:** You think others have high expectations of you and that they expect you to be perfect (regardless of whether this is true). You fear they will be critical of your performance if you don't do everything perfectly.

☐ **Dissatisfaction:** You have a tendency to feel like you're never "good enough." It's hard to meet the standards you set for yourself, so you're constantly dissatisfied and feel like something is not "right."

☐ **Reactivity to Mistakes:** You tend to experience negative emotions in response to real or perceived mistakes.

After reading through the list, reflect on any insights or observations that came up for you:

_____

_____

_____

_____

_____

Now, see if you can take a step in reversing some of your perfectionism by paying attention to the language you are using. In therapy lingo, we often refer to the concept of *mustabatory language*. (No, that is not an innuendo in there!) The idea is we often talk in "musts," "shoulds," and "have tos"—and this language reflects our perfectionistic demands. In addition, words like "always" and "never" can be a tip-off that you might have a tendency toward black-and-white thinking and perfectionistic tendencies. Over the course of the next week, see if you can try this one simple experiment. Nix these trouble words from your vocabulary and replace them with something more compassionate and understanding. Here are some examples:

- **Old Language:** I *have* to be on time to this movie or I'll miss the previews.
- **Reframe**: I'd love to make it to the movies on time as previews are my favorite part. But if it doesn't happen, it won't be the end of the world.
- **Old Language**: I *must* get the promotion and raise no matter what.
- **Reframe**: In an ideal world I'd get the raise. If it doesn't happen this time, I'll be disappointed, but maybe it'll happen the next time.

Record some of your examples from the past week:

_____

_____

_____

_____

_____

_____

Tool #7 | Perfectionism in the Pinterest Era

THERAPIST OVERVIEW

Never before in history has perfection been so ubiquitous for millennials than it is now on social media. Apps are readily available that allow people to airbrush their bodies, thin out their faces, smooth out lines, and do what was previously only possible with photo-editing equipment reserved for major magazines. Pinterest helps the crafty and aspiring DIY-ers flaunt their impossibly beautiful creations at the chagrin of millions more who tried those very projects and failed miserably. Reality TV stars create images of seemingly effortless wealth and resources as they laze about all day with professional hair and makeup artists pampering them until they get up to run an errand in their six-figure vehicle. One might say perfectionism in the millennial era is perfectionism on steroids.

Helping clients make sense of what is reality and what is altered is a critical aspect of the therapeutic work. To more seasoned therapists, reality is obvious, but for millennials who are particularly plugged in, their versions of reality may be highly skewed. After all, with browsers that track each user's activities—and that then show ads targeted particularly to them—a confirmation bias supports their worldview. When they log onto social media, they may be exposed to only one political agenda, or one way of eating and exercising, and wind up in a bubble all their own. In fact, you may come to hear from clients more and more about the "bubble" they live in. Standards of perfection exist and are aggrandized in each of these unique bubbles, and social media plays a huge role in perpetuating the stereotypes within. The following activity will help clients explore how they can overcome the pursuit of perfectionism on social media.

Perfectionism in the Pinterest Era

Duration: 30-40 minutes	**Frequency:** As Needed	**Level of Difficulty:** Moderate

Instructions: The next time you are tempted to post something, take a step back and see if you can refrain from editing, spending an excessive amount of time writing a caption, or creating hashtags.

If you aren't on social media, pick a facet of your life where you are particularly inclined to be perfectionistic. Maybe it is perfecting a recipe, doing your hair, or waxing your car to an exquisite shine. See if you can force yourself to do a half-hearted attempt at any of these things and see what happens. It may be painful at first, but you'll see that you survived—and not only that, it's likely you'll be far less anxious or distressed as a result. Record the challenge and your experiences below:

_____

_____

_____

_____

_____

_____

_____

_____

_____

_____

Tool #8 | Letting Go of Control

THERAPIST OVERVIEW

For millennials, issues with control can come up repeatedly as a therapeutic theme. As a generation that grew up with freedom of expression and a strong sense of self-efficacy, not having control is often a major concern for millennials. They may be so accustomed to essentially getting what they want, when they want it (often now!) that patience, waiting, and relinquishing control can be major barriers to their success.

Learning to surrender to lack of control is a major skill many millennials can benefit from mastering. Especially as millennials make the transition out of college or graduate school into the working world, the meritocracy to which they were accustomed may suddenly vanish. No longer do "A" grades result in academic scholarships or strong letters of recommendation. In the real world, nepotism, favoritism, and other perceived injustices abound, and letting go of control can help millennials mitigate the frustrations they may come to experience as a result.

To assist millennials with control issues, it can help to first identify the source and context of their need for control. Common reasons that individuals may develop control issues include anxiety, low self-esteem, fear of abandonment, traumatic or abusive life experiences, lack of trust, fear of painful experiences, perfectionism, or restrictive beliefs owing to cultural or faith-based expectations (Good Therapy, 2019). Once you have identified the source, it is important to recognize the symptoms of controlling tendencies, as these behaviors can manifest inwardly (e.g., eating disorders, compulsive exercise, compulsive cleaning, substance abuse, self-harm) or outwardly (e.g., bullying others, overprotectiveness, dishonesty, gaslighting, abusive behaviors).

In working with millennials, it can help to combine traditional approaches to control issues while maintaining unique aspects of the millennial experience in mind. For example, while it is important to assess and discuss general factors that could lead to control issues, you also need to keep in mind that, as a whole, millennials grew up in the era of helicopter parents. As the popular cultural quip of the "participation trophy" emerged during the millennial era, it is commonsensical that millennials are used to accolades, choices, and countless options. As a result, not having these external motivators or praise can further exacerbate control issues.

Tech Tip:
In interpersonal relationships particularly, control concerns are ever-present. Single millennials may be so accustomed to crafting the perfect text message or Snapchat that they may have no idea what to do when faced with a situation they cannot control. I cannot tell you how many millennial females I have worked with in therapy who say outright they want the "upper hand" or "final say" when texting a relationship partner. They simply cannot feel powerless or be a possible victim to a breakup, "ghosting" (when all communication is suddenly cut off by someone the person may have been casually or actually dating), or other unexpected scenario.

Letting Go of Control

Duration: 15-20 minutes	**Frequency:** As Needed	**Level of Difficulty:** Moderate

Instructions: Learning to let go of control can be a challenging task for any of us. But mastering this skill pays dividends as it helps you better roll with the punches and learn to "lean in" to challenges that come up in your daily life. As you know, a child's fever is out of your control, as is a company's decision to downsize and layoff individuals. The more you try to control, the more anxious you get and the worse you may treat yourself and others. Learning to keep your controlling tendencies at bay can allow for much more peace and contentment in your life.

To practice letting go of control, try any of these experiments over the coming weeks and months. Although some may seem silly and others downright impossible, learning to intentionally let go of control can be immensely beneficial.

- Go to a restaurant and don't read the menu. When the server arrives to take your order, randomly point to an item and let yourself be surprised.
- The next time you make a social media post, don't use a filter, don't use a hashtag, and don't try to control or distort how things appear in any way. Be completely unfiltered and transparent.
- When you're at the grocery store and the bagger asks you for paper or plastic, let them decide.
- When deciding on a movie to see with a friend, partner, child, or spouse, let them choose the film.
- When texting a friend regarding plans, let them be the first to make a decision or move. Don't try to influence or nudge them in any direction.
- Order your coffee as it comes. No modifications.
- Let the laundry pile up a few days more than you ordinarily might let it. And *try* not to sweat it.
- Don't do the dishes one day or don't pre-wash and put them in the dishwasher. Let the machine do what it is meant to do.
- If you are taking a flight and are in the habit of changing seats, don't. Stick with what you have and see what happens.
- If you're walking the dog and it wants to go in the opposite direction, just do it. See where you end up.

- If you are used to tailgating, swerving in and out of traffic to get ahead, or keep changing lanes, stop! Not only is it unsafe, but you can live with being in your car an extra five minutes. (You rarely end up getting that far ahead anyway.)
- When you use your GPS for directions and it doesn't give you the route you want, surrender and just take the route you are given.
- At a movie theater, church, or other venue with seating, don't focus on the "best" seats. Just sit wherever is easiest and most convenient.
- If your house has an alarm, see what happens if you don't set it one time. Likely, you will be just fine.

To continue gaining mastery over your need to be in control, consider the concept of *surrendering*. List the first five things you can think of in your life where surrendering might help decrease distress:

1. _____

2. _____

3. _____

4. _____

5. _____

Finally, as you will learn more in Part 4 of this book, consider mindfulness and meditation approaches to help you learn how to let go with ease and serenity.

Understanding Loneliness

THERAPIST OVERVIEW

For perhaps the first time in history, loneliness has reached epidemic proportions. More than half of adults in the U.S. experience loneliness, with younger generations being impacted the most (Cigna, 2018). When it comes to millennials in particular, 25% report having no acquaintances, 22% report having no friends, 27% report having no close friends, and 30% report having no best friends (Ballard, 2019). Millennials are naturally in the very heart of this epidemic, which has led experts to report on the disturbing irony that the social media generation is also the loneliest generation. Although many millennials are old enough to remember meetups that were not tech-mediated, they have quickly lost touch with the idea of using paper invites versus setting up a Facebook event and simply clicking "add" to everyone they know. It gives the semblance of plentiful friends, but what happens when only two people show up?

In these times of 24/7 connectedness, it may sound paradoxical that anyone would feel lonely. After all, clients are receiving "likes," comments, and feedback on social media, and they may be in a group chat or text thread that keeps pinging on their phone every few minutes. The reality is that as technology and constant availability has surged, so has loneliness. While millennials may feel proud of their hundreds of Facebook "friends" or even thousands of "followers" on Instagram, they quickly become aware of the superficiality of these virtual relationships in true times of emotional need. Whether it is a breakup, ill family member, or job loss, millennials need to have someone they can talk to on a deeper level. Someone they can have coffee with face-to-face, or at the very least pick up the phone and hear the voice of a good friend. Too often, the allure of a lengthy list of friends can lead to breadth (not depth) of relationships, which leaves millennials particularly vulnerable to loneliness in trying times. Understanding and having these discussions regarding loneliness is integral when conducting therapy with millennial clients.

Given the sheer amount of work that can be done involving loneliness and social connectedness (in real life as opposed to the virtual one), the following activity contains two parts. First, clients are asked to identify various types of loneliness that resonate with them. This helps get the conversation started, as loneliness can be a highly vulnerable area to explore. It can be embarrassing and even shameful for clients to admit to having very few, if any, friends at all.

Then, clients are asked to create a plan to combat each type of loneliness they've identified. As clients put together an intervention plan, it is crucial to encourage openness and frequently affirm the small steps they are taking in combatting their loneliness. For example, a millennial who freelances and frequently works from home may have few opportunities to make friends at work or even in their apartment complex. Coffee shops may be filled with people rapidly typing away on their computers, but it can also be inappropriate to disrupt them to stimulate conversation. So be sure to be flexible and realistic in suggesting interventions for branching out.

Tech Tip:

In the digital age, it is easy for individuals to forgo hitting up the movies with friends for a night spent watching Netflix at home alone (Davis, 2019). Furthermore, the age of technology has made flaking out on friends easier than ever before. Not in the mood for that meet-up? Just text to cancel—no calling and hearing the sound of disappointment in a friend's voice. When individuals need a pick-me-up, they no longer turn to friends but to technology. And over time, this leads to social circles that drastically dwindle in size. Being aware of these trends can help you better learn the intricacies of millennials' lives.

Understanding Loneliness

Duration: 20-30 minutes	**Frequency:** As Needed	**Level of Difficulty:** Moderate

Instructions: Happiness experts, including best-selling author Gretchen Rubin (2017), believe that loneliness is a major obstacle on the path to well-being and that identifying the source of this loneliness is a key factor in overcoming it. This list describes seven forms of loneliness. Put a checkmark by any that apply to you.

_____ 1. **New-situation loneliness:** This type of loneliness occurs when you are new to a school, city, or other environment.

_____ 2. **I'm-different loneliness**: This type of loneliness occurs when you are in a familiar setting, but you feel like you can't connect with those similar to you. Maybe you are the only person of color in a predominantly white neighborhood, or the only atheist in a sea of Catholics.

_____ 3. **No-sweetheart loneliness**: As it sounds, this type of loneliness involves a sense of yearning for a romantic partner. Maybe it is nearing Valentine's Day and the isolation feels particularly apparent. Or, perhaps all of your friends are in relationships and you feel like the third wheel.

_____ 4. **No-animal loneliness**: For those of you who grew up with animals or are pet lovers by nature, it can feel lonely when a beloved pet dies or you are in a living situation that does not allow animals.

_____ 5. **No-time-for-me loneliness**: A very common form of loneliness, this occurs when it feels as though others are too busy for you. Maybe someone relocated and they don't make the time to call you, or they have found new friends and you feel left out.

_____ 6. **Untrustworthy-friends loneliness**: Perhaps you have friends but don't know if you fully trust them or want to be completely open and honest with them. Many millennials have friends that turn on them or talk behind their backs, which can make it challenging to be vulnerable.

_____ 7. **Quiet-presence loneliness**: Maybe your roommates went away for a weekend and left you home alone, or your best friend is out of the country traveling without cell reception. There is a loneliness that comes from missing someone's presence. It doesn't mean you were always interacting with this person before but that there was a feeling of comfort and stability from having them around.

Once you have identified the types of loneliness that may impact your life, consider making an action plan. Pick two to three types of loneliness that you think you can concretely improve upon or make changes to.

For example, maybe you now moved into an apartment that allows cats, and for the first time you can actually entertain the idea of adopting a pet. Or, after taking some time to heal from a break-up, you're ready to consider online dating.

List the type of loneliness you want to work on and describe what steps you can take to improve the situation:

Loneliness Type:

_____

Action Plan:

_____

_____

_____

Loneliness Type:

_____

Action Plan:

_____

_____

_____

Loneliness Type:

_____

Action Plan:

_____

_____

_____

Tool #10 — Managing Loneliness

THERAPIST OVERVIEW

Many of you may have experienced this common scenario: You are at a party or other social gathering making small talk. You are laughing, nibbling on appetizers, and then go home feeling utterly empty inside. You were just with people, so what happened? While it may have been an initial boost to be around people, that isn't sufficient for feeling included in a group. The common adage that loneliness is cured by "putting yourself out there" may not work as a means of obtaining closeness. In fact, many well-intentioned efforts to put yourself out there can fail miserably and lead to worse consequences. Any therapist who has attended a very awkward "mixer" at a professional conference can attest to the fact that a room full of new people does not bring out the best in the most socially adept of individuals.

Therefore, physically surrounding yourself with people does not counteract loneliness. Loneliness can still happen in the presence of others. Rather, the *feeling* of closeness is what is key in combating loneliness. And we can develop this feeling of closeness by cultivating *caring* and *knowing* (Asatryan, 2016). Caring is more than concern for a friend's struggles, but really being invested in a friend's overall well-being and showing that they matter to you. Knowing involves more than just understanding the facts about someone. It involves having a true connection developed over time where you might come to know their likes and dislikes, and even read their mind on occasion.

In this next activity, clients will learn to manage their loneliness by brainstorming how they can better demonstrate caring and develop their depth of knowing with their existing friendships. Encourage clients to focus on only one or two key relationships, as this can serve them much better than instantaneously joining large groups of people.

Terminology Tip:
Among millennials, it may be common to hear the term "swiping left/right." This most often refers to the online app, Tinder®, which has become synonymous with many millennials as a "hook-up" app. The app essentially shows photos of individuals in one's geographical radius, and the user swipes left (if they aren't interested) or right (if they are), which then allows them to communicate through the app. For lonely millennials, Tinder can sometimes serve as an unhealthy coping mechanism. They may drink to excess when feeling lonely, go on the app, and meet someone who could potentially put them in a harmful situation. Many times, there is fallout involving shame and regret. Be aware of these trends with your millennial client. It is also helpful to note that these apps come and go, and there are countless popular platforms from Bumble® to Jdate® (for Jewish individuals). When you're uncertain of the specific terminology, don't be afraid to ask. They change all the time, and no one expects you to be thoroughly current on the latest dating apps.

Managing Loneliness

Duration: 20-30 minutes   **Frequency:** As Needed   **Level of Difficulty:** Challenging

Instructions: While we can't grow instant-friends, we can take an honest look at existing friends. Who is really there is times of need? What friendships are best to let go of? And which friendships have the potential to blossom into something much more? Write your reflections here:

_____

_____

_____

_____

_____

_____

Now, see if you can work on cultivating a greater sense of *caring* and *knowing* with the friends that are remaining. It doesn't mean you have to have deep, hours-long conversations all the time—just a few meaningful face-to-face interactions can do much to increase a sense of closeness. Caring goes beyond concern for a friend and involves truly being invested in them genuinely and wholeheartedly. Brainstorm a few ways you can demonstrate *caring* to your friends:

_____

_____

_____

_____

_____

Finally, brainstorm a few questions you might ask a friend to encourage your depth of *knowing* them. Knowing involves more than just facts. It has to do with understanding their likes and dislikes, their sense of humor, and what stories or books might resonate with them. These questions don't have to be too personal, just things that you think might help to bring you closer to one another:

_____

_____

_____

_____

_____

Learning Micro Self-Care

THERAPIST OVERVIEW

Fortunately for many therapists, millennials are already savvy to the notion of self-care. That said, it certainly doesn't mean they necessarily integrate it into their lives. Devices and technology are often used as a substitute for true self-care, or they impinge on time that would have otherwise been set aside for self-care. I will admit to countless times that I have gone on YouTube to practice yoga with my favorite teacher, only to get sidetracked by answering that one last work email and then see my 30-minute yoga time dwindle down to mere minutes. There have also been several times I've intended to open up the meditation app on my phone only to end up scrolling through feeds instead.

In her book, *Simple Self-Care for Therapists: Restorative Practices to Weave Through Your Workday*, Ashley Davis Bush (2015) describes the importance of engaging in macro and micro self-care practices. While the book is written with a therapist audience in mind, her strategies can undoubtedly be adapted for work with clients. Given that micro self-care is often easier for clients to tackle and integrate into their lives, it is covered in this tool first, followed by macro self-care in the following tool.

Micro self-care refers to practices clients can do on a daily basis that are highly effective in keeping them grounded and content. These include practices such as getting up from their desk and walking around, savoring a piece of chocolate in the afternoon with some coffee or tea, or listening to soft music or a guided meditation with their eyes closed. Micro self-care activities can be further divided into the grounding, energizing, or relaxing types. Grounding practices often dovetail nicely with mindfulness-based practices, as they include meditation, deep breathing, drinking a warm cup of tea, or taking a gentle walk outside to reconnect with nature. Energizing practices involve those that get the energy flowing, such as going on a brisk jog or walk, or even jumping up and down on a mini-trampoline (called rebounding). Relaxing practices typically involve spa-like experiences, such as taking a bath, lighting candles, using aromatherapy, or going to a sauna.

When discussing self-care conceptually with clients, it is important to distinguish between hobbies, self-care, and coping tools. Comparing and contrasting these practices can help clients learn more about the nuances of self-care so they understand what you are asking of them. The following Venn diagram can help elucidate the overlap and relationship between these concepts.

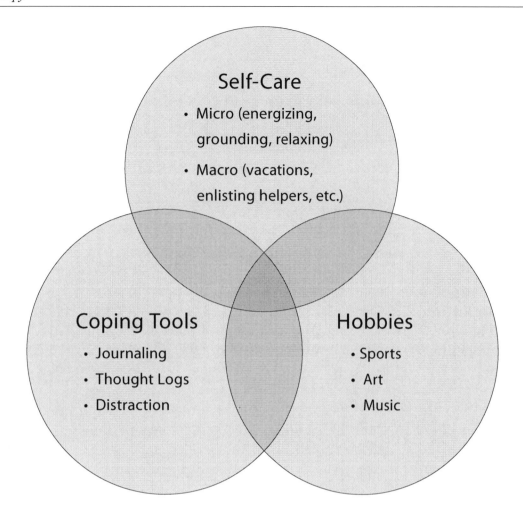

While it is important not to get too caught up in the nuances, it can help to recognize that some tools may fall into multiple categories. For example, listening to music can be a hobby, coping tool, and form of micro self-care. Taking a bath might be a form of self-care but not necessarily a hobby. A bath can also fit into an action plan from a coping tools checklist. Use this next activity to help clients identify micro self-care activities they can start incorporating into their daily lives.

Tech Tip:
As you discuss the concept of self-care with your millennial client, be sure to assess how technology plays into their routine. Countless millennials will report using Netflix or YouTube to unwind and truly equate watching a show with the concept of relaxation. Consider gently moving your client away from the notion that these habits represent self-care and, instead, encourage them to try a more active (stretching) or intentional (deep breathing, meditation) practice. Streaming a television show is often something clients are already doing, so don't be afraid to challenge them to really determine what self-care looks like when they're off their devices.

Learning Micro Self-Care

Duration: 10-15 minutes	**Frequency:** As Needed	**Level of Difficulty:** Easy

Instructions: Self-care can be thought of in two primary ways: micro and macro. In this activity, you will be asked to focus on micro self-care. These are the small daily touches you can add to your life that make a world of difference. In fact, you may already be well aware of the importance of self-care or may have been practicing small acts of self-care throughout your life. Maybe after a stressful day at work you opted for a yoga class instead of a bucket of popcorn and your favorite flick. Or, perhaps you schedule regular breaks to meditate or go for a mindful walk. Wherever you may be starting in your journey, learning to be intentional about integrating self-care throughout your daily life is an optimal way to maintain your overall well-being and happiness.

The list here identifies three facets of micro self-care: grounding, energizing, and relaxing. Read through the list and consider placing a checkmark by the self-care practices you already do and an X next to the ones you'd like to integrate into your routine.

Grounding Self-Care Practices

Grounding practices can be thought of as those that help us reconnect to our deepest selves. They can include the following:

_____ Drinking a cup of tea with warming spices, like ginger, cinnamon, or turmeric

_____ Connecting to nature by taking a walk in the park or simply going outside

_____ Tending to a garden or even an indoor plant

_____ Eastern practices, such as Tai Chi, Qigong, and yoga

_____ Gentle stretches that can be done at home on a mat or in your bed

_____ Using your five senses to connect to the present moment

Energizing Self-Care Practices

Energizing practices are those that uplift us when we feel overburdened by the demands of the world. These practices can energize but also soothe. Examples include:

____ Active forms of yoga, such as Vinyasa or Hatha

____ Taking a brisk walk in the park, or hiking by a river or meadow

____ Self-massage techniques that involve gentle tapping

____ Singing

____ Dancing

____ Cleaning and decluttering a space

____ Laughter! Keep a collection of stories, memes, or jokes to look at when you're stressed

Relaxing Self-Care Practices

Relaxing self-care practices are those we are most familiar with in our culture. You've probably seen images of someone stressed out soaking in a bath or at a spa. While these images may be readily available in your mind, the realm of relaxing self-care practices extends far beyond.

____ Sleeping, resting, or taking a nap, even if only for 10 to 15 minutes

____ Meditating, doing deep breathing, or sitting in silence

____ Using water to unwind (for example, taking a bath, lying by a pool, or trying out a floatation tank)

____ Using a mandala coloring book designed for adults

____ Giving yourself a spa treatment

Now, come up with your own personalized plan of micro self-care activities.

Micro Self-Care

In an effort to prioritize myself daily, I will commit to the following activities each week:

Grounding	Energizing	Relaxing

In an effort to set better boundaries so I can practice self-care, I will also prioritize saying no when appropriate (for example, to excessive social engagements that zap my energy instead of lifting my spirits).

Areas where I will set limits:

_____

_____

_____

_____

Because self-care also involves taking care of myself through nourishing foods, sleep, and exercise, I will also focus on the following goals:

Nutrition: _____

_____

Sleep: _____

_____

Exercise: _____

_____

Tool #12 | Learning Macro Self-Care

THERAPIST OVERVIEW

For many millennials, images of macro self-care run rampant in their social media feeds. They may see friends and family on lavish vacations laying poolside on a beach, or going on a retreat in a Costa Rican jungle. They may see influencers touting a "detox" experience in Thailand or visiting sacred temples in Bali. Self-care can be quickly equated with an expensive price tag that does not fit the typical millennial budget unless they are among the financial elite. The reality is that macro self-care doesn't need to be so far-fetched. It can involve scheduling a spa day, hitting up the golf course, or planning a fishing trip with friends.

Given that macro self-care is certainly more time-intensive, and can take planning to execute, many millennials struggle with such activities. These forms of self-care may feel removed from everyday life and hence can go unacknowledged. While it is easy enough to pour a cup of tea every afternoon and drink it mindfully, it can be more complex to schedule an all-day spa experience with a good friend (or to save up for that long-anticipated vacation). Naturally, these forms of self-care are not going to be daily occurrences, but they are still critical. They just require patience, persistence, and planning on the part of clients, and this is where a therapist's gentle guiding hand is essential.

For therapists, it can be challenging to help clients identify macro self-care goals, and it often takes some serious brainstorming to determine what is truly feasible in a millennial client's life. One way to approach this is to help them scale back more far-fetched "dreams" (e.g., 10-day silent retreat in Big Sur) to reality (e.g., attending a local two-day meditation workshop). Another simple tool is to use the four seasons to plan macro self-care activities. For example, fall might be an ideal time to spend a day at the pumpkin patch or apple orchard. Winter might be the perfect time to visit a tree farm, go skiing, or do other cold-weather activities that might be rejuvenating and readily available in their local area. As anyone who has simply spent one day away from work and immersed in nature can attest, it truly doesn't take much to feel energized when you take that time for yourself.

Millennial Vignette:
I recently worked with a millennial therapy client who was burning out under the pressures of a highly demanding career. Her personal life mirrored a rollercoaster ride, and we discussed her going on a vacation with her on-again, off-again partner to get some space to really evaluate the direction of their relationship. While this may sound unconventional, both partners had maintained a very close and enduring friendship during the "off" times of their romantic relationship. Nonetheless, as they both work demanding hours with little to no time off, a vacation was exactly what they both needed. As the client and I discussed this more, it became clear that this form of macro self-care could satisfy several of her needs at once: from giving her a break from work to devoting time to a loving relationship that she had little time for. In the end, they wound up reuniting, and she elected to take time away from work to pursue career goals more aligned with her true passions.

Learning Macro Self-Care

Duration: 10-15 minutes	**Frequency:** As Needed	**Level of Difficulty:** Moderate

Instructions: Macro self-care can be thought of as a major event that you may have been looking forward to, like having a spa day or hitting up the sauna with friends. It can involve going on an island vacation where you lay by the water all day (as opposed to following a strict and full sightseeing itinerary), or attending a spiritual retreat of sorts. While it may take some thought and planning, see if you can brainstorm ideas for macro self-care in your life. You might think of wellness activities offered through your gym, church, or even workplace to get you started. Or, you can go on Groupon® or other similar sites to find deals for pedicures, or simply a long overdue haircut (goodbye manbun!). List some of your initial ideas here:

_____

_____

_____

_____

_____

_____

_____

Now, see if you can schedule these activities monthly, if not quarterly. An easy way to remember the importance of macro self-care is to tie it to the seasons and holidays. Perhaps you do something to unwind after the stressors of excess family time at Thanksgiving or shopping for Christmas. You might slow down at a pumpkin patch or take a day to pick out a tree at a farm without checking your watch or phone every five minutes. Think ahead to spring break and schedule a possible beach getaway. Maybe you can finally hit up the golf course when the weather clears up in the summer, or you can finally get your skis out once the snow starts to fall.

Having a plan in place in advance can help you take advantage of the changing seasons and the unique opportunities they each provide. Otherwise, you can find yourself buried in work and other commitments while time keeps trucking on.

Fill out this chart with ideas for macro self-care that you can implement each quarter or season. Some key holidays have been included to jog your memory of fun macro self-care plans that might go with the seasons:

Fall (Halloween, Thanksgiving)	Winter (Christmas, New Year's, Valentine's)	Spring (Mardi Gras, St. Patrick's Day)	Summer (Fourth of July, Labor Day)

| Tool #13 | Integrating Alternative Therapies |

THERAPIST OVERVIEW

Given the rise in popularity of complementary and alternative treatments among millennials, it is important to recognize the utility of such approaches in the holistic treatment of clients. For some therapists, it may feel as though many millennial clients jump on every bandwagon of alternative treatments, ranging from essential oils for anxiety to kombucha to help their gut microbiomes, but there are in fact evidence-based advances in the alternative therapy domain.

According to the National Center for Complementary and Integrative Health (NCCIH), which is an agency within the National Institutes of Health (NIH), complementary modalities include (1) natural products and supplements, such as probiotics, herbs, vitamins, and minerals; and (2) mind-body therapies, including (but not limited to) yoga, acupuncture, massage therapy, chiropractic and osteopathy manipulation, Tai Chi, Qigong, relaxation practices, healing touch, and hypnotherapy. Remedies involving homeopathy, Ayurvedic medicine, ancient Chinese medicine, and naturopathy are also included on their list.

Therapists don't need to be well-versed in every modality, but they should maintain an open heart and open mind by integrating what they do know and by openly discussing what clients may be trying on their own. As many of us know, medical science is ever emerging with new findings and, at times, debunking old medical wisdoms. So if a client is rubbing essential oils on their feet to avoid the flu virus in lieu of getting a flu shot, being open-minded will certainly help the therapeutic alliance.

Millennial Vignette:

Openness and acceptance toward alternative therapies is an excellent way to instill hope in clients. For example, I worked with a millennial therapy client who was suffering from chronic pain that doctors could not explain. Unsurprisingly, this client was in great psychological distress because he had been to countless specialists and felt he couldn't get any more answers from doctors. We discussed the idea of letting go of the need to understand the *why* of pain and moving into coping, acceptance, and alternative therapies. We discussed how acupuncture might provide short-term pain relief, how meditation could ease anxiety and distress, and even how dietary changes could change the inflammation response in the body.

Terminology Tip:

In many parts of the country, CBD is having its moment, so to speak. Short for *cannabidiol*, it is an active ingredient derived from the hemp plant that many millennials swear by for depression, anxiety, insomnia, pain, and any other host of issues. It can be used topically, orally, and is now even in some makeup products. That said, research on safety and efficacy is severely limited. As a therapist who practices in states where cannabis is legal, this has brought forth much debate amongst practitioners regarding whether or not CBD use is acceptable among clients. As a result of legalization and normalization of such products by companies, there is little consensus regarding safety, addictive properties, and long-term health factors. Clinicians must ultimately use their own clinical judgement in assessing use and abuse of these substances. For the purposes of the following exercise, cannabis and CBD products have been omitted.

client worksheet

Integrating Alternative Therapies

Duration: 10-15 minutes	**Frequency:** As Needed	**Level of Difficulty:** Easy

Instructions: Complementary and alternative therapies predate modern medicine. From Chinese medicine to Ayurveda, ancient sages have healed using techniques that continue to endure to this age. Perhaps you already use some alternative therapies as an adjunct to your overall holistic wellness practice, or you have been itching to try something quirky and new like flotation therapy. (You may have seen those space-age looking pods filled with water at some point in time.)

On the list provided, place a checkmark next to the strategies you already use and an X next to ones you'd like to try. The next time you are looking for something to help lift your mood, see if you can turn to one of these alternative therapies.

_____ Acupressure

_____ Acupuncture

_____ Aromatherapy

_____ Autogenic training

_____ Ayurveda

_____ Chiropractic

_____ Cryotherapy

_____ Crystal healing

_____ Cupping therapy

_____ Ear candling

_____ Electromagnetic therapy

_____ Flotation therapy

_____ Hypnotherapy

_____ Ionic foot detox

_____ Music therapy

_____ Naturopathic medicine

_____ Negative ion therapy

_____ Nutritional supplements

_____ Osteopathy

_____ Pilates

_____ Qigong

_____ Reflexology

_____ Reiki

_____ Shiatsu

_____ Sound therapy

_____ Tai chi

_____ Thai massage

_____ Therapeutic horseback riding

_____ Therapeutic touch

_____ Transcendental meditation

_____ Trigger point therapy

_____ Traditional Chinese medicine

_____ Traditional Japanese medicine

_____ Traditional Korean medicine

_____ Traditional Mongolian medicine

_____ Traditional Tibetan medicine

_____ Visualization

_____ Other? _____

_____ Other? _____

Part 3

managing racing thoughts and rumination

Cognitive Behavioral Therapy

Cognitive behavioral therapy (CBT) is an empirically-supported treatment most commonly used for clients with anxiety and depression. Therapy-savvy millennials may not always know the ins and outs of this treatment, but they often request it by name given its efficacy and structured approach. Often known for examining the relationship between **A**ffect (feelings), **B**ehaviors (actions), and **C**ognition (thoughts)—known as the **ABC**s of CBT—this treatment can be a wonderful resource for information-hungry millennials. As they love to understand the *why* of an approach, CBT is fairly simple in its aim. Change can happen when goals are set to modify any part of the **ABC** cycle.

The tools presented in this section aim to highlight some of the key elements of CBT that can be of use to millennials. These interventions are somewhat more time-consuming than the SFT tools presented in Part 2, but they are just as essential. In order to manage worry and rumination, clients must have a strong command of core CBT concepts, such as identifying cognitive distortions, engaging in behavioral activation, and understanding emotions. These are the tools that many clinicians wish were taught in primary schools but that never quite make the curriculum.

In the section that follows, there are several handouts devoted to understanding cognitive distortions and tracking them using a traditional thought log. As conventional CBT often involves months of analysis of thought logs and patterns, this step is broken down across multiple activities for ease of use and explication. Additionally, simple but effective tools, such as journaling and goal setting, are included in this section. An infusion of millennial-specific concepts, round out this section to make it as relevant to this generation as possible.

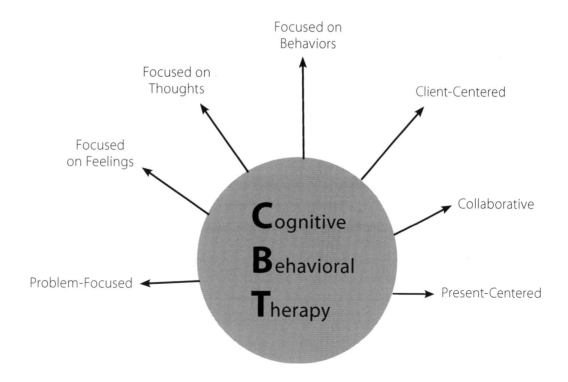

Tool #14 | Journaling 101

THERAPIST OVERVIEW

As many therapists are already well aware, research indicates the most commonly recommended therapy intervention by therapists is journal writing (Borkin, 2014). It not only helps promote self-soothing, but it also helps clients process and discover new ways to view situations. For many millennials, though, the concept of private journaling has become a lost art of sorts. Instead, social media has turned into a running public journal for this generation, where they profess everything from political beliefs to romantic relationship updates. Not too long ago, couples getting married made a splash as they "live tweeted" during their once-intimate ceremonies. No moment is too private to be shared. Whether it is learning of a birth or death, everything has become streaming commentary on a millennial's social media feed. Some do this to brag and keep up with friends, others to make exes jealous. Others are completely oblivious to their over-sharing, as it has become such a norm.

Instead of using social media as a way to memorialize major life moments, encourage millennial clients to take a step back and really process their emotions thoughtfully and intentionally with the help of a journal. Work with them to see how they can honor their own feelings and experiences, as opposed to broadcasting everything to the world. Given that clients will be asked to reflect on their emotions and experiences from this point forward in this workbook, starting out with journaling is an easy way to help them become more comfortable in processing through challenging feelings. A journal is also a useful tool to have as they try out new experiences and start learning to identify their triggers.

Tech Tip:

Many tech-savvy millennials may be eager to download yet another app on their phone when journaling is suggested as a recommendation. Challenge your client to using a traditional paper journal or notebook to record their thoughts. Modern journals even feature a code for added security if this is a concern for your client.

In-Session Tip:

Journals are one of my favorite ways to tap into the private thoughts of quiet and more introverted therapy clients. Of course, I never read their journals as this would definitely be intrusive and inappropriate! I just ask that they bring it into session to help jog their memory regarding important factors they want to discuss. For clients who might be more reserved or who get flustered in session and may not recall what happened the previous week, journals can be an excellent adjunct.

Journaling 101

Duration: 10-15 minutes	**Frequency:** Daily	**Level of Difficulty:** Moderate

Instructions: How many times have you been going about your day when suddenly an idea for a social media post popped up? Either you took a funny picture or thought of a witty line. Or, maybe you had a bad day and wanted to broadcast it to the Twitterverse in hopes of getting some positive or comforting feedback. Between all your posts and comments, you might even see your social media feed turn into informal therapy sometimes. It is natural to start thinking this is normal. The truth is, we all need some space, solitude, and privacy to really delve into our deepest emotions and experiences. Whether it is working through trauma or persistent anxiety, constantly broadcasting a play-by-play of our day to the world is not helping us in any way. Learning to sit down, even for a few minutes, each day to journal is a really powerful way to teach us to honor our feelings while also learning to identify our triggers and vulnerabilities.

Over the next week, experiment with keeping a *private* journal. Perhaps a loved one or friend gave you a journal as a gift one time, or maybe something caught your eye at a gift shop. Select a special journal where you can record your thoughts for this activity. Or, you can use the blank piece of paper included after these instructions. While there are certainly online apps that serve as journals, most clients find that the physical act of putting pen to paper is the most helpful. Once you have identified what you'd like to use as a journal, reserve a few minutes before going to bed to jot down some reflections, fears, hopes, or dreams.

Since journals can sometimes feel too open-ended, consider the following journaling ideas or prompts. Pick as many that feel right for you, and commit to journaling daily for a week.

✓ Keep an art journal or sketchbook to draw any feelings, ideas, or thoughts you might have.

✓ Consider keeping a "gratitude journal" where you simply list three things you are grateful for each day.

✓ Use your journal as a space to write down every single one of your worries and fears in the form of a "brain dump."

✓ Make your journal a place to write down inspirational quotes you come across or positive affirmations about yourself. Each day come up with a single quotation or affirmation.

✓ Write down a list of everything you did that day. It doesn't have to be long paragraphs, just a bulleted list of when you woke up, what you ate, what you did, who you talked to, and so forth. You can choose a number to rate how you felt about the day on a scale from 1 to 10, with 1 being awful and 10 being wonderful.

✓ Pick one of the goals you have been working toward in this workbook, and write about how your progress is coming along and how you might want to change things up to help you succeed.

✓ If you are currently in therapy or meeting with a counselor, consider writing down the things you might want to bring up at your next session. It can help jog your memory regarding what you wanted to talk about.

Journaling Space

_____

_____

_____

_____

_____

_____

_____

_____

_____

_____

_____

_____

_____

_____

_____

_____

_____

At the end of your experiment with journaling, answer the following questions:

What types of prompts did you find yourself most drawn to?

_____

_____

_____

Did you find a recurrent theme that came up in your journaling (e.g., a troublesome issue in your life or anxious feelings)?

_____

_____

_____

Did you find that journaling positively impacted your daily life in any way?

_____

_____

_____

How might you commit to journaling on a regular basis? Would daily or even weekly journaling be feasible in your life?

_____

_____

_____

Write down how often you would like to see yourself journaling and what type of journal you might keep (e.g., sketchbook or gratitude journal). If you haven't already done so, you might even consider purchasing a special journal or notebook for regular use.

_____

_____

_____

Tool #15 | Emotions Are More Than Emojis

THERAPIST OVERVIEW

Discussing emotions can be a challenge for many millennials. For those who are more professionally engaged and driven, it may be especially challenging, as they may have learned from parents, mentors, or peers to push down feelings and keep trucking on. In fact, it is no surprise that the concept of grit came to be heavily researched and popularized during the millennial era (Duckworth, 2018). While perseverance is key to long-term success, many millennials can burn themselves out, compromising the essential components of their well-being in the pursuit of excellence. When millennials experience emotional fallout—from panic attacks to tearful spells they can't always understand—this is typically an indicator that they've put some accomplishment ahead of their own emotional needs.

While there are certainly plenty of stereotypes regarding millennials as a coddled and overindulged generation, they are also recognized as a generation that was overscheduled and overburdened with the weight of needing to excel at a variety of extracurricular activities. Therefore, the concept of recognizing and honoring feelings can be a bit difficult to approach with many millennials.

You can help millennials start to discuss their emotions by adapting the classic feelings chart exercise with a lighthearted technological twist that involves emojis. Given the preponderance of emojis used by millennials—whether in text messages, emails, or on social media—these can be a natural springboard for discussing and tracking emotions. Process what emojis they use most frequently, or what emojis might be overused or might over-dramatize a situation. Whenever millennials struggle with answering the question of "how do you *feel*" about any scenario, it may in fact help them to identify what emoji they might use when describing the situation to a friend or partner.

In-Session Tip:
Learning to become more in tune with their emotions is a key skill for millennials to learn. While some millennials can be keen to do CBT as a means of skipping over the importance of feelings, and focusing on thoughts, it is important to remind clients that these elements work *together* and not separately. Millennials can be quite crafty at steering the focus of the conversation away from emotions, and being alert to this tendency can help you encourage them to listen to their inner voice and to the feelings they are likely pushing down. Other key signs to look out for are physical manifestations of distress (racing heart, fast breathing, crying) to which clients attribute no apparent trigger. It may take them time for them to start listening to their feelings and to learn to pay attention to the warning signs before emotional fallout occurs.

Terminology Tip:
An acronym that is ubiquitous among millennials is TMI. This refers to the notion of "too much information." Most commonly this is used colloquially as it might under any other ordinary circumstance to denote when one has overshared intimate details of their life or a scenario. It has gained popularity namely due to the rise of social media and tendency for individuals to overshare without even realizing it. When so many are posting and publicizing what used to be highly private events, norms have certainly become skewed. This said, it is also readily acknowledged by many when boundaries have been crossed and one has shared TMI…

Millennial Vignette:
I worked with a client once who reported frequent crying spells "out of the blue." She could not attribute the crying to anything in particular and even reported there were no feelings whatsoever attached to the tears. She was extremely worried about her symptoms and was concerned she would have to go on psychotropic medication. It took some processing to learn that she was so accustomed to having such a full plate that she was constantly on the edge of teetering and crashing down. She had learned to cope by just persisting, and she didn't see others struggling, so she considered her own reaction abnormal. We started tracking her mood, daily activities, and stress levels, and we also started working on removing individual plates from her towering stack. After several months, her tearful episodes (which used to occur daily) had reduced to once a week, and she sometimes went entire weeks at a time with no tears. She became involved in sports, which gave her a physical and social outlet, and we started working on time management as well. Not surprisingly, her fear of needing to go on medication went away altogether given her vast improvement.

Emotions Are More Than Emojis

| **Duration:** 10-15 minutes | **Frequency:** As Needed | **Level of Difficulty:** Moderate |

Instructions: It is not uncommon for many millennials to express discomfort with really talking about deep emotions. When you experience random "TMI" moments with friends, you may feel like some things are better left unexplored, or at least that's how it might seem at first. But the truth is, whether we have bouts of depression, concerns with self-esteem, or struggles related to trauma, we have to learn how to become comfortable acknowledging and discussing our emotions. The easiest way to start is through the use of emojis, which can also be a fun way to think about your feelings.

Over the next week, track the emojis you use most often to express any type of emotion, whether it is to friends, family, or co-workers. Draw them here:

Next, under each drawing, write down feeling words that describe what you are feeling when you use that emoji. For example, the heart-eyes emoji might signify feelings of love, warmth, or comfort. See how many different emojis you use and what the range is. Do you notice they are skewed in an overly positive or negative manner? If so, you might consider broadening your emoji vocabulary. Perhaps when you have had a tough day, instead of using the tears-streaming emoji, stick with one teardrop instead. And, for bonus points, start using feelings words instead, and minimize or get rid of emojis altogether.

After trying this activity out for a week, spend a few moments reflecting on this activity:

_____

_____

_____

_____

_____

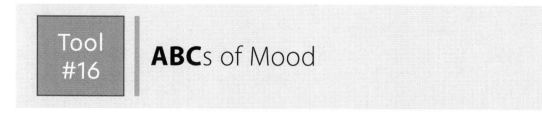

THERAPIST OVERVIEW

A simple and effective way to integrate CBT interventions with millennials is to begin by introducing them to the **ABC**s of mood: **A**ffect, **B**ehavior, and **C**ognition. This relatively easy-to-remember mnemonic can remind clients of how their thoughts, behaviors, and moods are all directly related to one another.

Generally, you can present this framework in any visual fashion you prefer. For example, the **ABC**s can be depicted via a triangle, circle, or other shape that denotes the relatedness of these factors. It can be helpful to draw out this cycle with clients in session to demonstrate how a stressful or upsetting scenario can be better managed by intervening at any point in the cycle. For example, if a client comes in and is tearful about a chaotic day of running late, spilling coffee, and staining their favorite shirt, it can help to start with their feelings or emotions (affect), then tackling how their thoughts (cognition) and actions (behavior) impacted this scenario. It might look something like this:

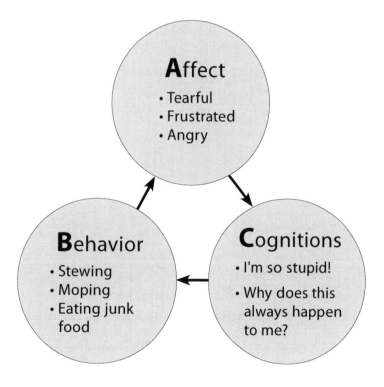

By reframing the scenario, the client may be able to change their thoughts or behaviors to diminish the severity of their emotions or to help the situation. This is not meant to invalidate truly upsetting feelings or force clients to find a silver lining. Rather, it is a proactive way of breaking down a scenario to make it more manageable and to allow for a more positive outcome. For example, the revised scenario might look something like this:

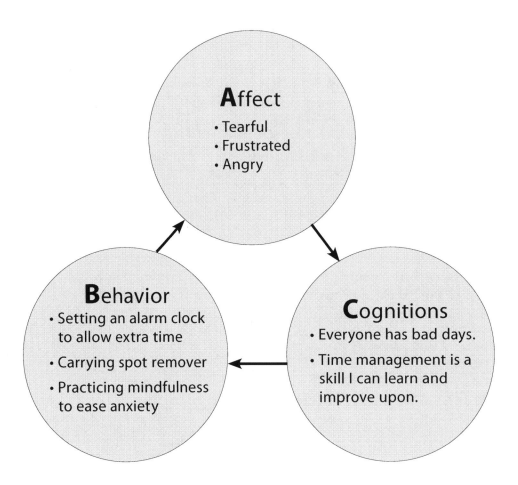

Demonstrating how this cycle works in session is a very impactful way to teach clients how to start reframing their most common triggers and challenges. They can also easily graduate to doing this on their own as they gain facility with this skillset. Learning to identify affect, behavior, and cognition is also a necessary first step before they move onto more challenging skills, such as identifying cognitive distortions. This simple rubric can familiarize them with the basic idea of reframing.

ABCs of Mood

Duration: 20-30 minutes	**Frequency:** As Needed	**Level of Difficulty:** Moderate

Instructions: When you change the way you react to a perceived problem, it can enable you to find relief faster than if you were to try to change the circumstances. While this process sounds a lot more complicated than it is, the field of cognitive behavioral therapy has some true gems when it comes to easing distressing thoughts. One of these gems has to do with the **ABC**s of mood. That is, the feelings and emotions (**a**ffect) we have in a given situation are closely related with what how we react (**b**ehavior) and what we think (**c**ognition) in response to that situation.

For example, if you receive your annual performance review at work and learn your work was rated as satisfactory or below, then you might feel very upset (affect), think you (or the boss) are not very bright (cognition), and not work as hard the next time a major project is due (behavior). Naturally, your thoughts, feelings, and behaviors are all related in this cycle. In CBT, the goal is to break this cycle so your mood and situation ultimately improve. The following diagram illustrates this relationship:

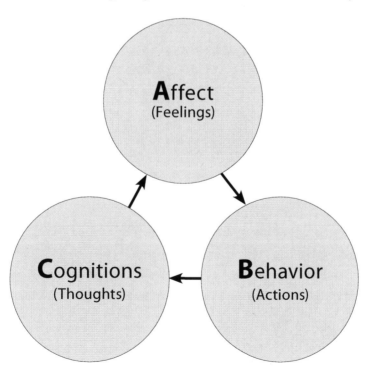

Using the same scenario involving a poor work performance review, you can break the cycle by targeting any part of the **ABC** triangle to improve the situation.

Affect: Feeling defeated, you decide to go for a jog to cool off and find that after 30 minutes or so, you are not nearly as upset and are feeling a bit more composed. Or, you talk to a colleague about the annual performance reviews and commiserate on how you both felt disappointed. You might journal to process your feelings or meditate to calm down.

Behaviors: Frustrated that the effort and overtime you put into your work was underappreciated, you approach your boss and ask for direct feedback about what went wrong. Or, you might ask to be paired with a senior staffer or mentor who could help coach you to do better in your role. If you have a boss with a reputation for being particularly tough, you might talk to colleagues about how to better work within your boss' managerial style.

Cognition: Instead of falling victim to defeating thoughts, you can choose to focus on the areas in which you are already doing well and realize this is only one performance evaluation that is meant as constructive feedback. You might consider the fact that you are new to the company and that it will take time for you to learn more about the culture and expectations of the workplace. You may consider that a poor evaluation does not equate with being fired and is a signal to improve rather than being unexpectedly let go from the company.

Now that you have a basic understanding of the **ABC**s, it's time to put these skills to practice with concerns that arise in your own life. Remember, it takes a lot of time and practice to change your thinking and approach to things. It is very normal to be reactive when something goes wrong. It will be a challenge to take a step back and realize that most of the problems that come up can be handled with relative ease. Using the **ABC** steps outlined here, come up with two to three scenarios from your own life (past, present, or upcoming), and go through the process of re-evaluating these scenarios:

Scenario: _____

_____

_____

Affect: _____

_____

_____

Behavior: _____

_____

_____

Cognition: _____

_____

_____

Scenario: _____

_____

_____

Affect: _____

_____

_____

Behavior: _____

_____

_____

Cognition: _____

_____

_____

Scenario: _____

_____

_____

Affect: _____

_____

_____

Behavior: _____

_____

_____

Cognarion: _____

_____

_____

| Tool #17 | Cognitive Disortions: Explained and in Action |

THERAPIST OVERVIEW

Fast-moving millennials have a never-ending dialogue of thoughts, ideas, criticisms, and analyses that runs on repeat in their minds (often at a million miles an hour). Much like their rapidly responsive technology, many millennials operate on turbo speed. Some may even talk at a lightning-fast pace, trying to fill you in on every last detail pertaining to a concern they may be experiencing. For a therapist, this can be the stuff of processing gold, but more than just being a soundboard, it is critical to teach millennials to examine their thinking patterns—especially the toxic and distorted ones—so they can improve their emotional well-being.

Especially for millennials who may be involved in social media, there can be a constant pull toward certain cognitive distortions, such as mind reading what others think when they post an Instagram story, or catastrophizing when they accidentally hit "reply all" on an email they were blind-copied on. Given that millennials grew up in the wake of many real tragedies—from 9/11 and school shootings to other terrifying daily realities—it is no wonder their minds can wander into negative thoughts. The world around them can be filled with triggers and real dangers. Helping them to come back to a state of balance and even neutrality in their own life circumstances is one of the biggest gifts you can give them.

Often considered the bread and butter of CBT, identifying and challenging cognitive distortions is one of the most powerful tools for working with clients. Learning about the numerous types of cognitive distortions can initially be overwhelming, so clients may find it comforting to know that they aren't the only ones who frequently fall into these traps. When used sparingly, you can use self-disclosure to demonstrate or share examples that normalize how we can all think in these ways. For example, it is very common to catastrophize after watching the evening news, or to magnify a careless driver's offenses while minimizing that job promotion you just got. These are all easy and neutral examples to share.

At the same time, help clients understand that when cognitive distortions increase in frequency and intensity, it can interfere with their emotional well-being. So while it can be normal for a client to "mind read" what their neighbor thinks about them from time to time, when they start to truly believe that everyone hates them, it is a sign of more serious trouble. Therefore, clients must learn to identify and challenge these thinking patterns so negativity doesn't take over their life.

Working through cognitive distortions presents a certain degree of intellectual challenge and can be quite time-consuming, so it is important not to overwhelm your client. Depending on the readiness of the client, it can be easiest to spend the first several weeks helping your client familiarize themself with the terminology presented in the following handout (Cognitive Distortions Explained). As they become more comfortable, you can introduce the second handout (Cognitive Distortions in Action) so they can begin catching themselves whenever they fall into a thinking trap. That being said, many times when a client is clearly following along and excited to do more, it can be completely appropriate to follow up by sending them home with the additional tools to complete over the course of several weeks. Use your judgment when deciding what will work best for your client.

Throughout the course of your therapeutic work, continue to help your clients by pointing out whenever you see them engaging in any of these thinking errors. Of course, be mindful that you are not confrontational about the errors you see. Instead, adopt a genuinely inquisitive and engaged mindset regarding their thought patterns.

In-Session Tip:
Catching cognitive distortions as they occur in session is an excellent way to either introduce this concept or simply reaffirm what has already been discussed. As therapists, we can become quite attuned to patterns in our clients' thinking. They may frequently use black-and-white thinking and expect perfection while constantly forecasting the future. When they provide examples of cognitive distortions in session, this is an excellent time to process and interpret their insights when it comes to their thinking patterns. In this manner, this exercise doesn't need to be an overly formal psychoeducational briefing but can naturally flow as an outgrowth of the clinical work you are already doing.

Millennial Vignette:
Teaching clients how to identify and challenge cognitive distortions is honestly one of my favorite things to do as a therapist. When clients are able to see—often for the first time—that they are not alone in falling into these thinking patterns, they express extreme relief and a sense of a burden being lifted off their shoulders. Other times, they giggle knowingly. I have had the unique opportunity to work with many elite student athletes throughout the years. One common theme I have observed is how the very things that helped push them to excel athletically and academically have also been their Achilles' heel. The tendency to engage in black-and-white thinking (I'll either rank first in my sport, or fail altogether), expecting perfection (I must execute my performance flawlessly), catastrophizing (if I don't make the Olympic trials all of my efforts have been for naught), and minimizing (all my track records don't mean anything special) are all very common. It can be a relief for such clients to learn they can break these thinking patterns that may have been drilled in their heads by coaches and parents and that they can still succeed—without all of the pressure.

Cognitive Distortions Explained

Duration: 20-30 minutes	**Frequency:** As Needed	**Level of Difficulty:** Challenging

Instructions: It is common for everyone to engage in distorted thinking patterns from time to time. These patterns of thinking are sometimes referred to as thinking traps or cognitive distortions. However, if you get into a thinking trap that persists across time, it can cause you to feel anxious or sad all the time. You might engage in some of these thinking patterns out of habit, or you may have learned them from your parents, but learning to spot these distortions is key. It can help you unlock the shackles of persistent negative emotions.

Read the following list of cognitive distortions and think about how they might pertain to your life. In the second part of this exercise, you will be challenged to come up with one example of each distortion as it applies to your own life. The categories listed here can have some overlap, so the goal is less to find the "perfect" fit for a distortion (which would be a form of distorted thinking itself!) but to start recognizing these patterns of thinking at large.

Black-and-White Thinking (also called All-or-Nothing Thinking)

In this type of thinking, you don't see the shades of gray or alternative possibilities in a situation. Things tend to fall into one of two categories: good versus bad, or success versus failure.

Distortion:

- You failed your annual performance review and will be fired.
- Your girlfriend didn't text you when she said she would, so she must be out with another guy.

Reality:

- Even if you did poorly on your evaluation, you're likely to be put on probation or given some type of warning instead of being erratically fired.
- It's possible your girlfriend ran out of battery on her phone and forgot her charger at home.

Catastrophizing

This distortion involves looking only at the worst-case scenario or expecting a disaster to occur.

Distortion:

- A political candidate you strongly dislike is elected to office and you assume disastrous consequences will occur.
- You have just finished reading about superbugs and start worrying excessively about taking vitamins, avoiding germs, and staying away from anyone who coughs near you.

Reality:

- While political candidates certainly do wield power, they are not dictators, and our justice system is set up with checks and balances. The policies that one candidate enacts can often be undone by their successors.
- While it is possible that you might catch a superbug, the actual probability is low given the percentage of people who truly become infected. Furthermore, becoming needlessly anxious can compromise your immune system and put you at more real risk than living your life in a healthy and balanced way without anxiety.

Fortune-Telling (Mind Reading or Predicting the Future)

This type of distortion involves jumping to negative conclusions either by mind reading or predicting the future.

Mind Reading Distortion:

- Your girlfriend responded to your last message with one emoji when she is typically more expressive. You assume she has lost interest in you and is messaging other guys.
- You brought your boss his favorite type of coffee and his reception was not as appreciative as you'd assume, so you start wondering if he doesn't like you very much.

Fortune-Telling Distortion:

- Given your girlfriend's minimal text, you assume she is going to break up with you soon.
- Because of your boss' lack of appreciation, you anticipate getting let go from the company.

Reality:

- Your girlfriend could have been busy and preoccupied with work when she texted you back.
- Your boss could be anxious about the financial projections for the company and may be having a tough time with his wife at home, so he was not intentionally unappreciative.

Mental Filtering

In this distortion, you selectively pay attention to the negatives and underappreciate the positives in a scenario.

Distortion:

- You throw a party and everyone on your invite list comes except for one of your best friends. Instead of focusing on the many other people who came, you dwell on the absence of one friend.
- You make a post on social media that gets dozens of positive comments, but one person leaves a negative and critical message. Instead of appreciating all the compliments and kind words, you focus on the one negative (and likely unhappy) person's message.

Reality:

- If you allow yourself to enjoy the party with those who are excited to attend, you will have much more fun than if you focus on the one friend who may have showed up but in a negative mood.
- Social media trolls will always exist and love having a platform for their negativity. Even though you may know that logically, it is important to focus on messages from real people who know you instead of anonymous, mean-spirited people.

Overgeneralization

Assuming bad things will happen repeatedly is a hallmark of this thinking trap. Individuals who tend to fall into this type of thinking will often use words such as "always," "never," "should," "must," "everyone," and "no one."

Distortion:

- You get invited to your friend's bridal shower on the other side of town and immediately start worrying. In your mind, you will never find parking, you always get stuck in traffic crossing the bridge, and these events never end up being fun.
- Your apartment lease is up, and you need to find a new place to live as your rent is going up. You start complaining that moving is always a pain, neighbors are a nightmare, and no one ever volunteers to help you.

Reality:

- Carpooling with friends, calling an Uber® or Lyft®, and leaving lots of time can help you be more relaxed when you arrive so you can actually enjoy yourself at the event.
- While often stressful, finding a new place to live can be an opportunity to explore a neighborhood you've been interested in, and you can even upgrade parts of your living situation. Maybe you can swing splurging for a loft, a pet-friendly place, or score some new friends among neighbors.

Emotional Reasoning

In this type of thinking, there is a tendency to mistake feelings for real facts.

Distortion:

- You go on social media and see an influencer you follow looking fit and glamorous. You immediately feel inadequate and inferior, and start thinking you need to lose weight and get a makeover.
- You feel butterflies in your stomach before an event and assume it will go poorly as a result.

Reality:

- Feelings of inadequacy do not equate with actual inadequacy.
- Butterflies are a perfectly natural response to new stimuli where there is uncertainty.

Personalization

This distortion involves taking responsibility or blame for things over which you may have little or no control at all.

Distortion:

- You invite your friends out for a birthday dinner, and as you are ordering, you realize your recently vegan friend has very little food options from which to choose. You spend the rest of the meal feeling guilty for having chosen a bad restaurant.
- You are working on a tight deadline with a team and the power goes out, causing you to lose all the work you were doing and setting back your ability to complete the project on time. You apologize to your boss repeatedly for the power outage.

Reality:

- It is impossible to know everyone's dietary restrictions, or to know the restaurant meal options everywhere.
- Severe weather and electrical outages can never be predicted. Further, while time management can help with last-minute deadline crunches, they are not always feasible when working with teams.

Expecting Perfection

This distortion involves having unrealistic expectations of perfection in your life.

Distortion:

- Every time you scroll through your Instagram feed, you feel a bit depressed as you look at how everyone is living these exciting, vibrant lives—while also looking beautiful.

- You have been training for a 5K for the last few months when you injure your hamstring. You become frustrated and upset that you can't run the race to the best of your abilities with your injury.

Reality:

- Social media shows the highlight reel of everyone's lives. Individuals can spend hours creating the "perfect" photo at the right angles while using filters to boost images. The truth is that this simply isn't anyone's reality.
- Injuries can happen to the most elite athletes and hinder their performance. No one runs a perfect race each time, nor is it practical. Weather, road conditions, and countless other uncontrollable variables contribute to race performance.

Self-Defeating Comparisons

This distortion involves inaccurately comparing ourselves to those who appear better off than we are and putting ourselves down in the process.

Distortion:

- You log onto Facebook to find former high school classmates and see whatever happened to them. You see several have gotten married, had babies, started their own businesses, and appear to be thriving. You look at your own life and feel badly about your outcomes.
- You are in your final year of law school when you learn one of the young professors at your college just received tenure. You feel behind in life and frustrated.

Reality:

- True success in life is measured across decades. There are countless famous celebrities, authors, and politicians who were unknown in their quarter-life years, only to become household names now.
- Comparing ourselves to those years ahead of us, whether chronologically or professionally, is rarely a fair comparison. Many times, life factors, finances, and a host of other variables impact professional outcomes rather than pure merit and grit.

Labeling

This distortion involves making a global, negative assumption about yourself based on one situation or experience. When you engage in labeling, you put yourself down instead of finding ways to remedy the situation in a way that betters your life.

Distortion:

- You get passed up for that job promotion and think to yourself, "I'm such a loser."
- Your boyfriend breaks up with you and you say, "I'm ugly and unlovable."

Reality:

- There will be other opportunities for promotions, and not getting one is not grounds to believe you're a loser.
- One breakup does not determine your self-worth, nor does it validate the truth of any negative thoughts you have about yourself.

Magnification/Minimization

This distortion involves discounting the good and overemphasizing the bad.

Distortion:

- Your phone just did an automatic update that lost all your fitness data. You become angry and stressed out (*magnification*).
- You just set a running record on your fitness app and downplay what an accomplishment this was because the data wasn't recorded (*minimization*).

Reality:

- Fitness is good for us regardless of what our data does or does not say. Sometimes our devices can actually make the things we enjoy, such as running, stressful because of technological errors.
- Even though your phone didn't record your workout results, it is important to celebrate small victories when they occur instead of over-focusing on technological glitches.

Cognitive Distortions in Action

Duration: 20-30 minutes	**Frequency:** Weekly	**Level of Difficulty:** Challenging

Instructions: Now that you have learned many different forms of cognitive distortions, see if you can come up with one example for each type of distortion using examples from your own life. It may take a while to recognize the distortions or inaccuracies in your previous thinking patterns—after all, these patterns may have been ingrained for some time—so take your time and be kind to yourself. If you struggle to find examples, feel free to reach out to family, friends, and even co-workers to see if they might be able to offer up some examples they may have noticed.

Once you identify a scenario, write it down and challenge yourself to come up with a statement that explicates the true reality of the situation. If you struggle with this part, reach out to your therapist or other trusted individual to help you think through it. Be sure not to ignore or skip the ones you are struggling with, as these are often the sneaky culprits that are harder to identify but ring true in your life nonetheless.

Black-and-White Thinking (All-or-Nothing Thinking)

Distortion:

_____

_____

_____

_____

Reality:

_____

_____

_____

_____

Catastrophizing

Distortion:

_____

_____

_____

_____

Reality:

_____

_____

_____

_____

Fortune Telling (Mind Reading or Predicting the Future)

Distortion:

_____

_____

_____

_____

Reality:

_____

_____

_____

_____

Expecting Perfection

Distortion:

_____

_____

_____

_____

Reality:

_____

_____

_____

_____

Mental Filtering

Distortion:

_____

_____

_____

_____

Reality:

_____

_____

_____

_____

Overgeneralization

Distortion:

_____

_____

_____

_____

Reality:

_____

_____

_____

_____

Emotional Reasoning

Distortion:

_____

_____

_____

_____

Reality:

_____

_____

_____

_____

Personalization

Distortion:

_____

_____

_____

_____

Reality:

_____

_____

_____

_____

Self-Defeating Comparisons

Distortion:

_____

_____

_____

_____

Reality:

_____

_____

_____

_____

Labeling

Distortion:

_____

_____

_____

_____

Reality:

_____

_____

_____

_____

Magnification/Minimization

Distortion:

_____

_____

_____

_____

Reality:

_____

_____

_____

_____

THERAPIST OVERVIEW

Thought logs are a mainstay of CBT treatment that help clients pull together all the tools they have been learning in therapy. It is an excellent way for clients to combine their new understanding of cognitive distortions with everything they have learned regarding the overarching connection between thoughts, feelings, and behaviors. Each log provides the client an opportunity to generalize their learning to other stressful scenarios, many of which involve the same negative thinking patterns. For example, if one log focused on how a client overcame their anxiety related to a blind date (e.g., catastrophizing, fortune telling), they could apply their action plan from this log to future anxiety-provoking situations. Although it can take clients some time to get into the habit of doing these logs, once they do, it can supplement therapy work beautifully.

Some millennial clients might want to use their phones or other form of technology to complete their thought log, especially given that there are countless mood apps available. However, encourage clients to start with a traditional written log, like the one provided in this workbook, before they move to a tech-centered version. When you have a handwritten sheet, it is easier for the client to process with you in session, and it also allows you to include a copy of the log in the client's file. Further, it can be therapeutic for many millennials to move away from their reliance on technology and to instead go back to the basics. As technology can also be a cause of stress for millennials, from being unable to resist the lure of checking their feed to navigating the frustration of an app constantly crashing on them, thought logs can easily be included as a part of a self-care routine. You might consider encouraging your millennial client to take a bath, to wear something comfortable or cozy, and—with no other distractions—to truly focus on completing their thought log in quiescence. This type of ritual can be both relaxing and reflective. Remind clients of the importance of completing one log each week for several weeks, if not a full month or more. Millennial clients particularly can be prone to quickly moving on to the next thing, so encourage persistence and routine.

Finally, it is very helpful to run clients through some sample thought logs. You can use a simple example to demonstrate how to use the log, or ideally pick a scenario that has been discussed in therapy as a part of the client's presenting clinical concern. One example I use frequently is a pop quiz, as the anxiety related to this scenario is universally understood and experienced by many millennials. A second example I often use is waiting to hear back regarding some important news—such as a job offer or admission to graduate school—where there is less control on the client's part. These sample logs are presented next.

Thought Log

Duration: 20-30 minutes	**Frequency:** Weekly	**Level of Difficulty:** Challenging

Instructions: Use the following log to integrate everything you have been learning about identifying feelings, the **ABC**s of mood, and cognitive distortions. By using the log, you can track any emotionally challenging scenarios that come up during the week and come up with an action plan. Ideally, you should complete this activity as often as possible so your ability to identify your thinking errors gradually becomes second nature.

Further, this sheet can be a helpful tool to use with a therapist to help track your mood over the course of treatment. Together, you can identify triggers, negative thinking patterns, and positive coping tools you can use in future scenarios. Many times, a second set of eyes can help you identify thinking traps you may not have even been aware of.

There is no correct "order" in completing the sheet. You can start with a difficult scenario and then list your feelings and thoughts in any order that they come up. Not every automatic thought will apply directly to a cognitive distortion, and that's okay. The idea is to get it all down and sift through your thoughts and feelings so you can identify your thinking traps and develop an action plan that will help you feel better.

sample client worksheet

Thought Log

Stressful Scenario: Pop quiz in organic chemistry class

Feelings	Automatic Thoughts	Cognitive Distortion	Alternative Thought and/or Action Plan
Fear Anxiety Dread Anger Frustration Panic Annoyance	I'm going to fail. I'll never get into medical school now. I hate this professor, he is such a jerk. Everyone is more prepared than I am. I wish I'd been keeping up on the readings more. I just wasted tuition money on a course I'll have to repeat. I'm so stupid!	Black-and-White Thinking Predicting the Future Self-Defeating Comparison Expecting Perfection Catastrophizing Labeling	The professor could curve the quiz, and I could still get a passing grade. Med school admissions are based on more than one grade on one exam. Next time I'll read reviews before picking a professor. I'll stay up on the readings going forward, and this won't happen again. I don't know yet that I've failed the whole course. I was unprepared, not stupid.

Stressful Scenario: Waiting to hear back about a job at dream company

Feelings	Automatic Thoughts	Cognitive Distortion	Alternative Thought and/or Action Plan
Anxiety Worry Hopelessness Yearning	What if I just blew the interview? This is the job of my dreams. If I don't get it, I'll be crushed. I feel this pit in my stomach about the whole thing. I must have blown it! I'm going crazy just sitting here thinking about it!	Catastrophizing Expecting Perfection Magnification Emotional Reasoning	There will be other jobs, and a better position could open up. I will keep looking at their site for new postings so I can be the first to apply to their next job. While I might be disappointed, the work culture may have turned out to be less than ideal. Or, I can talk to others who work there to see how I can boost my chances next time. Just because I feel anxious, it doesn't mean I didn't get the job. I'll call my best friend who is a good listener. Then, I will go for a light jog or do a yoga class to help ease my anxiety while I wait.

client worksheet

Thought Log

Scenario: _____

Feelings	Automatic Thoughts	Cognitive Distortion	Alternative Thought and/or Action Plan

Moving Beyond FOMO and YOLO

THERAPIST OVERVIEW

Many millennials have grown up with the popular acronyms FOMO (fear of missing out) and YOLO (you only live once). These terms harken to millennial idealistic aspirations of living one's best life and not standing on the sidelines of the action. Naturally, the surge in social media platforms and activity has acutely heightened—and is likely largely responsible for—the concept of FOMO. Millennials often are very aware of what everyone is doing at any given moment and can be overwhelmed by the variety of options at their disposal. Or worse, they may feel intense loneliness when they are excluded from such activities and feel like they're living on the outside looking in.

The concepts of YOLO and FOMO have real consequences for millennials' lives. They may spend excessively on lavish vacations and bridal showers in keeping up with the Instagram lives they see and end up in debt. Or, they may feel a need to take advantage of every opportunity available to them while single or childless and burn themselves out. Even worse, there are cases of Peter Pan Syndrome (Kiley, 1983), which has existed far before the millennial generation was in the period of emerging adulthood. They may refuse to grow up, fueled by a combination of economic factors limiting upward mobility and a peer group who is emotionally in a similar space as them.

Fortunately, the concept of affective forecasting is highly instructive in alleviating many of the FOMO moments that millennials experience. Research on affective forecasting has found that we often make poor predictions about how things will make us feel in the future. That is, our ability to anticipate (or "forecast") the impact of future events on our mood is deeply flawed (Gilbert, 2007). Learning to become a more accurate "forecaster" of our mood is a challenging skill to learn but can pay dividends over time.

Introducing this concept therapeutically can be quite simple. Have clients think back to a major event in their lives that they spent months anticipating. Maybe it was getting their first real adult job with benefits or buying a car that was new instead of an old junker. Was it everything they had imagined, or were circumstances different from what they had thought? Maybe the job turned out to be filled with political office drama. Or, perhaps everything went smoothly, and they were in bliss for weeks. Then something happened and the magic slowly died down only to be replaced by some new anticipation or stressors of life.

Discussing the idea of affective forecasting and how we can over-anticipate or misjudge the real impact of a scenario on our lives at large is a helpful tool for millennials. In this activity, they can start tracking major life events—both those that occurred in the past and those that are upcoming—to start setting realistic expectations that can impact their long-term happiness.

Moving Beyond FOMO and YOLO

Duration: 15-20 minutes	**Frequency:** As Needed	**Level of Difficulty:** Moderate

Instructions: *Affective forecasting* is an important concept in happiness research that involves predicting how we believe we'll feel in the future. Research into this phenomenon has found that, as humans, we're often poor "forecasters" when it comes to our mood. That is, we're not great at anticipating how things will make us feel in the long run. Have you ever said to yourself, "If this thing happens, I'll be so happy that I'll never want anything again"? Chances are that if your desire came true, after a few weeks or even months, you acclimated to your new normal and were no longer on cloud nine as you thought you would be. This is what scientists often call *hedonic adaptation*, the idea that we return to our previous emotional state after a major event. This can relate to both positive and negative events. If you ever bombed an exam, you may have been devastated, but after a few weeks, your emotions were back to normal.

Learning to identify errors in our thinking and in our ability to predict events is a powerful way to reframe events and check our expectations. As many millennials report, mood can sometimes feel like a rollercoaster ride. One day everything is going amazing, and the next it feels like everything is coming crashing down. By taking a step back and comparing these highs and lows to previous experiences, you can learn to take charge of your emotions and finally get off the emotional rollercoaster.

To get into the habit of becoming a better mood forecaster, first take out your planner, calendar, or phone and find some key life events that happened over the last several months. Maybe you forgot about the beach trip you took a month ago or the GMAT exam you were dreading for the last six months. List two scenarios on the spaces provided, one for a positive event and one for a negative event. Then, using the rating scales provided, circle how you thought the event would impact your mood, how it actually impacted your mood, and how you feel now that the event is in the past. A sample scenario is provided for you first.

Sample Scenario: _____ Taking the GRE exam _____

Anticipated Mood

Highly Stressful	Somewhat Stressful	Neutral	Positive	Highly Positive
①	2	3	4	5

Actual Impact on Mood

Highly Stressful	Somewhat Stressful	Neutral	Positive	Highly Positive
①	2	3	4	5

Current Mood Regarding Past Scenario

Highly Stressful	Somewhat Stressful	Neutral	Positive	Highly Positive
1	2	③	4	5

Negative Scenario:_____

Anticipated Mood

Highly Stressful	Somewhat Stressful	Neutral	Positive	Highly Positive
1	2	3	4	5

Actual Impact on Mood

Highly Stressful	Somewhat Stressful	Neutral	Positive	Highly Positive
1	2	3	4	5

Current Mood Regarding Past Scenario

Highly Stressful	Somewhat Stressful	Neutral	Positive	Highly Positive
1	2	3	4	5

Positive Scenario:_____

Anticipated Mood

Highly Stressful	Somewhat Stressful	Neutral	Positive	Highly Positive
1	2	3	4	5

Actual Impact on Mood

Highly Stressful	Somewhat Stressful	Neutral	Positive	Highly Positive
1	2	3	4	5

Current Mood Regarding Past Scenario

Highly Stressful	Somewhat Stressful	Neutral	Positive	Highly Positive
1	2	3	4	5

After rating your anticipated mood versus your actual and current mood for these past scenarios, use what you've learned to better forecast events coming up in the future. List one positive event you are very excited about, as well as something you are not looking forward to. Rate how you think it will impact your mood, and then brainstorm some ideas on how to appraise the scenario in your mind. An example is provided first:

Positive Scenario: <u>For my birthday, my boyfriend bought my tickets to a concert to see my favorite band. It's going to be the highlight of my summer.</u>

Anticipated Mood

Highly Stressful	Somewhat Stressful	Neutral	Positive	Highly Positive
1	2	3	④	5

Appraisal: <u>The event will definitely be fun, and I'm very excited. In addition to the anticipation, I'm going to focus on savoring the experience and having gratitude for this amazing gift. I'm also going to be prepared for the possibility that not everything will go according to plan, and that is okay.</u>

Positive Scenario:_____

Anticipated Mood

Highly Stressful	Somewhat Stressful	Neutral	Positive	Highly Positive
1	2	3	4	5

_____

Appraisal: _____

_____

_____

_____

_____

_____

_____

Negative Scenario:_____

Anticipated Mood

Highly Stressful	Somewhat Stressful	Neutral	Positive	Highly Positive
1	2	3	4	5

_____

Appraisal: _____

_____

_____

_____

_____

_____

_____

Tool #20 | STRENGTHS Chart

THERAPIST OVERVIEW

Charts are a handy way for millennials to start connecting their behaviors with their mood and are an excellent tool to use early on in therapy. Behavioral activation interventions can be particularly impactful for millennials struggling with depression and anxiety and can help them feel empowered that they are taking control of their mood and well-being. Too many times, clients report seeing a therapist and never having been given a single handout to help with their mood.

Although there are countless charts available for clients use pertaining to behavioral activation and mood tracking, the **STRENGTHS** chart included here is simply one iteration of this. It can be easily adapted for use among a variety of populations, including millennials, and is a key tool in any therapist's arsenal, as it is quick, simple, and highly impactful. The chart simply asks clients to track the following **STRENGTHS** throughout the week: **S**leep, **T**ime Management, **R**elaxation, **E**xercise, **N**utrition, **G**ratitude, **T**hought Logs, **H**obbies, and **S**ocial Time. By paying attention to these essential building blocks of mood, millennials can start to set goals and track how they impact their overall well-being.

When discussing this handout with millennials, it can be helpful to emphasize that goals be **SMART** (**S**pecific, **M**easurable, **A**ttainable, **R**ealistic, and **T**ime-bound) so they can see small successes. You might have them place a sticker in each box when they complete the activity to bring a sense of fun and nostalgia to the activity. There may be resistance to particular activities, but emphasize the importance of completing each section. The activity they are resistant to is typically the one they need to work on the most. At the same time, be gentle and ease into more challenging goals. For example, if a client is feeling depressed and is socially isolating, it can be acceptable to have them make a phone call or send a text message to start with. Ideally, over time they can move to a FaceTime call with an old friend, a face-to-face coffee meet-up, and a more outgoing excursion.

Furthermore, explain to clients that this chart can help them identify patterns in terms of which activities boost their mood. For example, in the sample chart provided with the activity, the client had markedly better mood on the days they exercised and slept well. They might have experienced a boost in positive emotions on the day they saw their friend and then felt motivated the next day to do even more feel-good activities. Showing the relationships between activities and mood helps clarify the overall goal of the activity. Note that there are online apps that can serve similar functions. While you don't necessarily want to discourage clients from using these apps, perhaps let this chart serve as a bridge to such technologies in the future.

Finally, this chart can also be an excellent barometer to track activities and mood across several weeks and see whether or not there is improvement. Many times, clients come in torn about going on antidepressant or other medications. I have often used this chart to make sure they are eating, sleeping, and exercising regularly before jumping to medication as the solution. Of course, clients who are severely depressed may have no energy or motivation to do any of these activities, but for clients who are generally functioning well and considering medication, a few weeks of trying the **STRENGTHS** chart first can provide excellent data to use in consultation with a prescribing provider.

STRENGTHS Chart

Duration: 20-30 minutes	**Frequency:** Daily	**Level of Difficulty:** Moderate

Instructions: Some of the key building blocks of positive mood and overall emotional well-being include the following:

Sleep

Time Management

Relaxation

Exercise

Nutrition

Gratitude

Thought Logs

Hobbies

Social Time

A simple way to think about it is that these factors help build your emotional **STRENGTHS**. When we have all these factors in check, we are far more resilient and able to deal with the unexpected turns life may have in store for us. Attending to your **STRENGTHS** will undoubtedly bring greater balance and joy to your life and help you get back to your normal self again.

On a Sunday evening, sit down in a quiet place to reflect on your goals for the week. Think realistically about goals you want to set for your well-being. Given that you will continue to hone and refine your desires for improvement, start simple. Don't set a goal to run a 5K if you haven't laced up your running shoes in months. Start with a 10- to 30-minute easy jog instead. At the end of each day, mark your mood on a 1-10 scale to help you track your progress. A sample log is provided, followed by a blank log you can fill out with your own goals.

sample client worksheet

STRENGTHS Chart

Target Behavior	How Often?	Mon.	Tues.	Wed.	Thurs.	Fri.	Sat.	Sun.
Sleep: Get 9 hrs	3-4x/week	X			X	X		X
Time Management: Use planner!	Daily			X				
Relaxation: Meditation apps	Daily	X			X	X		X
Exercise: Jog	3x/week	X			X	X		X
Nutrition: Drink more water	4x/week		X		X			
Gratitude: List 3 things I'm grateful for	Daily	X		X	X	X		
Thought Logs: Complete therapy homework	Daily		X		X		X	
Hobbies: Practice guitar	Daily			X	X			X
Social Time: Coffee with Anne	2x/week			X	X			
Mood Rating (1 = Horrible, 10 = Excellent)		6	3	8	9	8	6	8

STRENGTHS Chart

Target Behavior	How Often?	Mon.	Tues.	Wed.	Thurs.	Fri.	Sat.	Sun.
Sleep:								
Time Management:								
Relaxation:								
Exercise:								
Nutrition:								
Gratitude:								
Thought Logs:								
Hobbies:								
Social Time:								
Mood Rating (1 = Horrible, 10 = Excellent)								

Tool #21 | Behavioral Activation Coping Tools List

THERAPIST OVERVIEW

For many millennial clients, who grew up during an era of extreme competition for a very limited number of internships and jobs with low pay, the concept of hobbies can be a very foreign one. Although contemporary culture may poke fun at millennials for living with their parents under limited economic prospects, the truth is that most millennials have been brought up to multitask numerous responsibilities without an understanding of how to wind down or take time to attend to their own emotional needs.

When the lifelong message for many millennials has been to do as much as humanely possible (cue: FOMO problems), it can take some time for them to remember the hobbies and activities that bring pure enjoyment to their lives. Often, they are so accustomed to spending what little leftover time they have with friends or on their devices, that suddenly it's been years since they finished a good book or picked up a guitar. Reintroducing millennials to long-lost hobbies can be an incredible way of providing them with very real interventions that they can start implementing from the very beginning of therapy. Unlike many other CBT interventions, which take time to explain and process, exploring new hobbies and returning to old standbys takes very little additional work while also helping clients feel like they're making true progress.

Furthermore, the beauty of this particular intervention is that it pairs very well with the introduction of coping skills. While distraction should not be the foremost intervention that any client learns, it is an excellent tool to use during times of crisis, or in the event of more severe depression. When handed an exhaustive list of activities they can try, it is unlikely clients will be unable to find something to do. Even if they complain of low energy or motivation, simply sitting outside on the front porch is a small but powerful way to implement change. Walking the dog, journaling, or doing any number of the activities listed on the worksheet requires little commitment but is an impactful way to engage in the therapeutic process.

In-Session Tip:

The interventions listed here can be an excellent means of helping clients distract themselves from a crisis situation in a productive and positive way. Whether clients are prone to unhealthy coping behaviors, such as using alcohol or drugs, or even suffer from disordered eating behaviors, having them turn to at least two or three of the activities listed here can create enough time and distraction that it may discourage them from partaking in more harmful coping behaviors. For example, if a client is prone to bingeing and purging or smoking marijuana on a regular schedule, you might suggest that the client do a few yoga stretches, read a magazine article, and get some fresh air before determining whether or not they can forgo the unhealthy coping skills to which they are accustomed.

Millennial Vignette:
One factor to note with this activity is that given how accessible it is, it can also serve as a barometer for client resistance or more severe concerns. For example, I once worked with a millennial male client who presented with severe depression and refused to do any activities on the list. He reported no interest in any of the activities nor any motivation to engage in any of them. Upon further assessment, it became evident that he was also a heavy drug user who was often under the influence during sessions. In this case, his resistance was partly influenced by his substance abuse, and I referred him to a comprehensive substance abuse treatment program aimed at reducing his problematic use rather than engaging in a futile battle to get him to use positive coping tools he had no interest in. It was a very valuable lesson that taught me not all clients are ready for our favorite therapeutic tools. But fortunately, this itself is a highly valuable form of information. Not all clients will love our interventions, and their refusal or inability to engage in these tools can help us hone our diagnostic skills as well.

Behavioral Activation Coping Tools List

Duration: 10-15 minutes	**Frequency:** As Needed	**Level of Difficulty:** Easy

Instructions: Below is a list of activities and potential ideas millennials can turn to for coping. Place a checkmark next to any activities you already participate in and an X next to the ones you are willing to try. Then, add any other activities you can think of.

____ Journal.

____ Write a gratitude list.

____ Go to a yoga studio and try out a new class.

____ Create a sacred space and meditate.

____ Go to a place of worship and pray.

____ Visit a Buddhist center or other spiritual place.

____ Go to a gym to exercise.

____ Lift weights.

____ Go swimming.

____ Take a Pilates or spinning class.

____ Ride your bike.

____ Go for a hike or plan a hike.

____ Go camping or plan a camping trip.

____ Go skiing or snowboarding, or plan a trip to a local mountain.

____ Dance in your room or take a class.

____ Rebound/jump on a trampoline.

____ Go for a run or jog outside.

____ Take a slow, meditative walk outside in nature.

____ Take a class in Tai Chi or Qigong.

____ Take your dog for a walk, or borrow a friend's dog and take it for a walk.

____ Go outside for fresh air, even if you just sit on the front porch.

_____ Go outside and watch the birds, animals, and nature.

_____ Join a game being played at your local playground, or simply watch the game.

_____ Play a musical instrument or learn how to play one.

_____ Sing or learn how to sing.

_____ Write or compose a new song.

_____ Write a poem.

_____ Learn a new language.

_____ Listen to upbeat, happy music.

_____ Make a playlist of uplifting songs for when you might need it.

_____ Sing in a local choir.

_____ Participate in a local theater group.

_____ Go to the movies.

_____ Make a list of your top five funniest films to watch when feeling down.

_____ Join a club.

_____ Make a fresh cup of tea or coffee, or a smoothie, and drink it somewhere special.

_____ Go to a new coffee shop or a favorite one.

_____ Go to a bookstore or library.

_____ Go to the mall or other shopping center to window-shop.

_____ Visit an arts and crafts store for supplies to start a project.

_____ Knit or crochet, or learn how to.

_____ Make a scrapbook.

_____ Take photographs.

_____ Draw, color, or doodle in your sketchbook.

_____ Color a mandala or other meditative image.

_____ Visit an art museum.

_____ Create a new recipe and try it.

_____ Sign up for a cooking class.

_____ Go out for something to eat.

_____ Cook your favorite dish or meal.

_____ Bake cookies for a friend in need.

_____ Sign up to volunteer for a charitable organization.

_____ Plant a garden or visit one.

_____ Clean out your closet and donate clothes you no longer wear.

_____ Organize your bedroom.

_____ Light candles.

_____ Take a relaxing bath.

_____ Take a warm shower.

_____ Give yourself a facial.

_____ Polish your nails.

_____ Get or schedule a pedicure.

_____ Go to a sauna or steam room.

_____ Schedule a haircut or try a new hairstyle.

_____ Get a massage or rub your own feet.

_____ Do a puzzle.

_____ Reread your favorite book or series.

_____ Read a magazine.

_____ Sleep or take a nap.

_____ Eat dark chocolate. (It's good for you!)

_____ Make a list of ten things you appreciate about yourself or that you are good at (and look at this list when you feel blue).

_____ Write a loving letter to yourself when you are feeling good and read it to yourself when you're feeling upset.

_____ Make a vision board.

_____ Other: _____

_____ Other: _____

_____ Other: _____

_____ Other: _____

Part 4

grounding frantic energy

Mindfulness-Based Therapies

For many millennials, mindfulness has become a popular buzzword of sorts. While some may truly understand the concepts related to this practice, others may not know how to apply it to their own lives. In its greatest simplicity, mindfulness simply involves maintaining a nonjudgmental, moment-to-moment awareness. It involves drawing your attention to the here and now and letting go of any judgments or expectations that you may have about the moment. Although mindfulness has its origins in ancient Buddhist meditation practices, it was popularized in Western practice by scientists such as Dr. Jon Kabat-Zinn, and it has become increasingly embraced as a therapeutic modality.

Guided by seven key principles, mindfulness involves the following elements: non-judging, patience, beginner's mind, trust, non-striving, acceptance, and letting go. For millennials in particular, these principles are true therapeutic jewels. Millennials often attempt to control things that are out of their hands, lack patience and trust in things working out, and have a hard time letting go of perfection, the past, and the need to constantly strive for more. Needless to say, mindfulness could easily have been created for millennials more than anyone.

Throughout this section of the workbook, you will find a variety of tools aimed at breaking down key mindfulness concepts in an easily digestible manner for millennial minds. The tools start out by explaining the seven principles of mindfulness through the use of millennial-specific examples and scenarios. Then, clients are encouraged to start adding in small moments of mindfulness throughout their day. Whether it is spending five minutes mindfully sipping a morning beverage, or being mindful in the shower or on their daily commute, they are introduced to mindfulness in small steps. From there, they are challenged to start integrating moments of meditation into their routine. They might start in their comfort zone by using an app to guide them through a meditation, but they will ideally move up to seated forms of quiet practice. They will also learn tools that pair naturally with the concept of mindfulness, such as the practice of self-compassion and yoga. Finally, the exercises conclude with some key elements traditionally used in dialectical behavior therapy (DBT) that can be of use during times of distress.

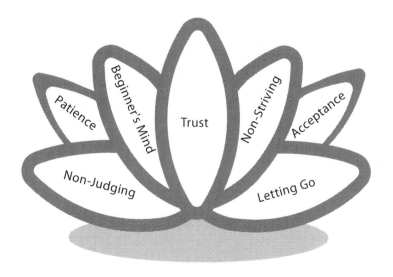

Tool
#22

Seven Principles of Mindfulness

THERAPIST OVERVIEW

Mindfulness is a buzzword that many millennials are familiar with. Maybe it's an influencer touting the advantages of a meditation practice, a morning ritual, or a mindful session of journaling. That said, even though many millennials are familiar with mindfulness as a general idea, they are not familiar with the core foundations of this practice. In fact, what mindfulness is, how it is defined, and what "counts" as mindfulness appears to get muddier all of the time.

Dr. Jon Zabat-Zinn, one of the founding fathers of mindfulness, describes the seven basic principles of mindfulness as non-judging, patience, beginner's mind, trust, non-striving, acceptance, and letting go. Naturally, there is much to unpack here. Any discussion with clients can begin with an overview of these principles, and each facet can be further explored and elucidated on a weekly basis. Having this overall framework can be exceedingly useful when processing stressors or other challenging circumstances in a client's life. Do not underestimate the power of reminding clients to be patient with themselves, or to not judge themselves or their circumstances. The explanatory handout provided here is a strong go-to sheet, as clients (and therapists, for that matter) need to regularly be reminded of these tenets of mindfulness.

Once clients conceptually understand mindfulness on deeper basis, they can transition more easily into determining what mindfulness looks like in their own life. Maybe there are aspects of mindfulness they have already incorporated into their routine through previous self-exploration and growth, whereas other concepts need more integrating. They can also begin using the log provided at the end of the exercise to help them approach life challenges using mindfulness principles. As different clients may take more to one approach or another—for example, a CBT thought log versus a mindfulness-based therapy log—it can be useful to determine what feels like a better fit for each individual.

Seven Principles of Mindfulness

Duration: 20-30 minutes	**Frequency:** Daily	**Level of Difficulty:** Challenging

Instructions: Dr. Jon Kabat-Zinn is one of the top researchers and experts in mindfulness. He describes the seven principles of mindfulness as: non-judging, patience, beginner's mind, trust, non-striving, acceptance, and letting go. Each of these concepts is described here with an accompanying example. In the pages that follow, try to come up with examples from your own life that describe how you might put each of these principles into action. At the end, you will find a mindfulness log to help you continue practicing these principles throughout your week.

Non-Judging

The concept of non-judging can be thought of as viewing events that occur from the perspective of a third-person omniscient narrator. Such a narrator typically reports things from a neutral, nonjudgmental position and does not get swept up in drama. They witness events but do not judge them as good or bad. They simply are what they are. Non-judging can be very difficult to practice, as we judge our experiences all day long. We feel good or bad, and then we make judgments about whether or not our experience is acceptable. Non-judgment asks us to simply witness without expectation, judgment, or preference.

Example: You see a post on social media that features a photo of three of your friends at a party you were not invited to. You immediately judge what they are wearing, judge whatever they are doing in the photo, and make assumptions that may not actually be fair or true. You are about to judge yourself for not making the invite list, when you realize you have been denying invitations for months. They likely thought you were not interested in attending. You realize you may have been unfairly judging your friends and that there may be more to the story than you were open to considering.

Your example involving non-judging:

_____

_____

_____

_____

Patience

For millennials, cultivating patience can be extremely difficult. Time may feel as though it is moving painfully slowly, especially when we are feeling discomfort. We want the bad feelings to go away quickly and become impatient and upset when they linger longer than we want them to. Patience allows things to unfold in their own divine time.

Example: It seems like all of your friends are either coupled, married, or having babies. They might even own a home or be well on their way toward one. Meanwhile, you feel like you are treading water, going from one relationship to the next, barely enjoying your job, and feeling frustrated. Practicing patience (and finding the silver lining) can allow you to make the most of being single and having the freedom to experiment with jobs and vocations until you find your passion. You have your whole life to "adult," and while you wait for things to settle down in life, you can find time to engage in new hobbies, get some exercise, create an art project, or do other rejuvenating activities.

Your example involving patience:

_____

_____

_____

_____

Beginner's Mind

Adopting a beginner's mind is akin to seeing things through a child's eyes—for the first time ever. It is similar to the old adage "stop and smell the roses." So often, we rush past the rose bush on our way to the bus stop that we don't notice its beauty. It is only when we stop one day that we can realize its beauty and fragrance for the first time. Having a beginner's mind allows us to get out of our ruts of thinking.

Example: You finally moved to the big city but are overcome by traffic, the high cost of living, and the other challenges that come with urban life. However, you also miss out on the diverse experiences and cultural immersions that surround you. Maybe one day on your walk to work you stop and take in an urban garden a few blocks down, or you remark at how you can drop by the local coffee shop without fighting for parking. Or, you simply notice storefronts, streets, and parks you'd never paid attention to before. See if you can experience your neighborhood like a tourist might.

Your example involving beginner's mind:

_____

_____

_____

_____

Trust

This principle involves trusting your intuition, your sense of self, and what it is that you need. Too many times, millennials can get caught up in what their friends, colleagues, and family are doing, and they ignore what is the best decision for themselves. Trust involves knowing your limits and being comfortable setting boundaries and taking time to nurture yourself.

Example: You get a text message from your friend in Human Resources that layoffs might occur. You start to worry about your work ethic, your reputation, and those projects you got in just under the wire. But then you also remember the concept of trust. You trust that you have a strong, open relationship with your boss and that even if you are laid off, it might be a sign the organization was not the best fit for you.

Your example involving trust:

_____

_____

_____

_____

Non-Striving

In today's ultra-competitive environment, there is much pressure placed on individuals to succeed. They must get the best jobs, earn the highest pay, and outperform their peers. This becomes such a deeply engraved mindset that the idea of non-striving can be completely foreign. In fact, it might even be confused with laziness! But in actuality, non-striving is about accepting things as they happen. It is the idea of allowing things to fall as they may without striving to change things.

Example: Your older sister was just made partner at a major law firm while you're getting weekly rejections from jobs you've applied for. You start to feel sorry for yourself and possibly even try to escape your misery through harmful behaviors, such as drinking. But in thinking about the principle of non-striving, you realize you are doing the best you can and that your unique talents will lead you where you are meant to be. All you can do in the meantime is continue to apply for jobs, work hard, and be kind and compassionate to yourself and those around you.

Your example involving non-striving:

_____

_____

_____

_____

Acceptance

Acceptance means allowing things to be as they are. Many times, we do not agree with things, but learning to accept them opens the doors to finding peace. If you are very politically active and find that your favored political party is not elected, then you might be unhappy, but you must learn to accept it. By pushing, denying, and trying to force things your way, only more struggle and strife arises. Acceptance allows us to still remain engaged and active, but it does not put us in a constant state of discomfort.

Example: You just went on Snapchat and learned your ex-boyfriend is dating someone new. You start crying and feel sad, rejected, and angry at him for moving on so quickly. Even though you are tempted to cyberstalk the new girl and send him angry messages, you realize the most peaceful way to exist is to accept that he has moved on. It may take you time to move on as well, but accepting this new state of affairs is more healing than is yearning for the past.

Your example involving acceptance:

_____

_____

_____

_____

Letting Go

Letting go can be extremely difficult in a culture where we so strongly desire to control our outcomes. A major component of Western culture involves being industrious and creating our own destinies. While this is a highly revered idea, it often leads to the common misconception that we can control all aspects of our life. This can lead to much despair when we are unable to control something. Learning to let go gives us the freedom to step back and close a door with the knowledge that a new one will eventually open.

Example: You are video chatting with your girlfriend and checking your social media feed when you see a photo of her with another guy at a party. You confront her and tell her you don't want her conversing with any guys other than yourself. However, you then come to realize that you cannot control who comes up and talks to her and that you can't control whether or not they end up in a photo together. All you can do is trust in the authenticity and openness of your relationship and let go of the idea that you can control her and all of her actions.

Your example involving letting go:

_____

_____

_____

_____

Mindfulness Log

To continue practicing and integrating the principles of mindfulness into your daily life, consider keeping a log of moments when you are tempted to numb yourself or escape. Using the log provided here, describe what happened and what thoughts and feelings came up. Then, write down which mindfulness principle would be helpful to remind yourself of in this situation, and consider what self-care strategy you could use to alleviate any discomfort you may be experiencing.

Scenario:

_____

_____

Feelings	Thoughts	Mindfulness Principle	Self-Care Action Plan

Tool #23 | Attitude of Gratitude

THERAPIST OVERVIEW

One of the most robust findings from the field of positive psychology is the importance of gratitude in facilitating happiness and emotional health. Fortunately for most therapists, the concept of gratitude gets plenty of face time in the millennial era. From workout tanks and mugs to artwork proclaiming words such as "#blessed" and "start each day with a grateful heart," millennials are very familiar with the importance of gratitude. That being said, it can be easy for many people to pay this concept lip service, treating it as a trend rather than a way of life. For example, many millennials may save their expressions of gratitude for the public sphere only. If their lattè art is particularly impressive, they may use this as an opportunity to boast (and share) how grateful they are for the simple things in life, as opposed to taking a mental picture and privately savoring the experience. Teaching millennials to think of gratitude as a small "thank you"—one that is given solely to the universe—can nudge them away from these public proclamations and teach them what authentic gratitude is really about.

In order to get millennials into the habit of practicing gratitude, you can use the very popular and well-researched gratitude intervention involving the "three good things" gratitude journal. Studies have indicated that journaling or listing three things individuals are grateful for each day can significantly increase happiness and improve their overall satisfaction with life (Emmons & McCullough, 2003). The activity provided here builds off this work and challenges millennials to start focusing on the positives they find in their daily lives. Doing so will not only improve their mood, but it can also go a long way in helping them become mindful and appreciative of small moments throughout their lives.

Social Media Tip:

Millennials are prone to using hashtags such as #TBT (throwback Thursday) or #latergram (for past photos they never got around to sharing) on their social media feeds. These are often used in conjunction with posts that may be used to express gratitude for a past vacation, to boast about college days of yore, or to show off photos of when their toddler was a newborn. While there may be no ill-intention behind these posts, it can come across as inauthentic or trying too hard. Why not revisit old photos privately and savor those moments instead of being inclined to share them with others? Discussing these factors with your millennial client can be useful.

Terminology Tip:

The term *humble brag* has become increasingly common among millennials. Stemming from the social media realm, the term is used when someone attempts to appear modest while actually seeking recognition and praise. For example, a millennial may post what is a known as a *selfie* (a photo they took of themselves), in which they look glamorous but remark they are not actually wearing any makeup. Or, they might post a photo of themselves volunteering at a homeless shelter with a caption that reads, "The real heroes are the homeless individuals." Humble brags can also appear as masked expressions of gratitude. For example, a wealthy individual might post a photo of their opulent home after a power outage and say how they feel #grateful.

Attitude of Gratitude

| **Duration:** 5-10 minutes | **Frequency:** Daily | **Level of Difficulty:** Easy |

Instructions: Modern day woes can quickly add up and leave us feeling tired, grouchy, or downright distressed. As the popular saying goes, "When it rains, it pours," and we can easily see how this applies to our own lives. However, research suggests that simply keeping track of three good things that happen to us each day for a week or more can have a profound impact on our happiness. While this practice may feel difficult at first (or it may start off easy and become more difficult as time goes on), it can be extremely powerful. In addition to increasing your overall sense of gratitude and contentment, it can make you aware of all the small miracles that happen in your daily life. You may find yourself becoming more mindful of how wonderful that sudden burst of sunshine felt on your skin during your lunch break, or you may truly savor that small slice of cake you found in the breakroom. All small victories, including anything that is cause for a mini-happy dance, count!

To get you started, use the spaces provided to start tracking three things you are grateful for each day over the next week. You can use a notebook or journal if you want to provide more detail, or you can make it as simple as bullet points. The key is to try something and stick with it.

Day 1:

_____

_____

_____

Day 2:

_____

_____

_____

Day 3:

_____

_____

_____

Day 4:

_____

_____

_____

Day 5:

_____

_____

_____

Day 6:

_____

_____

_____

Day 7:

_____

_____

_____

At the end of the week, reflect on any overall observations you may have made:

_____

_____

_____

_____

Finally, reflect on whether you might be willing to commit to this practice for two weeks, a month, or maybe more.

_____

_____

_____

_____

Tool #24 | Self-Compassion

THERAPIST OVERVIEW

For millennials struggling with depression, anxiety, or any other mental health concerns, self-compassion can be a challenge to practice. While they may instinctively understand what it means to be compassionate toward other people or other causes, turning this kindness toward themselves can be more challenging. Upward social comparisons, which run rampant on social media, can certainly exacerbate things. When millennials are already feeling down, many may turn to technology to feel better, only to end up feeling worse when it appears everyone is doing better in life than they are. This can make practicing self-compassion seem like a futile endeavor, as they may not believe they are worthy or deserving of such self-care.

However, the importance of self-compassion cannot be understated. Self-compassion researcher and expert Dr. Kristin Neff has found that self-compassion is more important than self-esteem, as it allows for a greater sense of emotional resilience, increased caring, and less anger and narcissism. In contrast to self-esteem, which is often contingent on external achievements and accomplishments, self-compassion allows clients to fully embrace who they are in a way that is not contingent on striving. They accept themselves just as they are. This leads to greater happiness, optimism, and overall life satisfaction.

The three primary components of self-compassion include: **(1)** self-kindness (not being harsh or critical of oneself), **(2)** recognizing one's humanity (realizing that humans are inherently flawed and imperfect), and **(3)** mindfulness (maintaining a nonjudgmental awareness). These elements are further explored in the activity that follows, which provides a short version of Neff's (2011) self-compassion scale to help clients start thinking more critically about their own self-compassion and how they may improve upon it.

Terminology Tip:

You might hear your millennial client use the term "slay" or "slaying it." I'll be the first to admit how surprised I was to see such an otherwise gruesome term be used in a positive context. The notion of "slaying" can refer to a number of things—many millennials use it to connote beauty and looking amazing. Others use it to refer to being on point with something or being very successful, such as the adage "nailed it" or "killed it." Keep this concept in mind, as many millennials struggle to cultivate an attitude of self-compassion when it seems like everyone around them is "slaying it" while they are consumed by their perceived inadequacies or failures.

Self-Compassion

Duration: 30-40 minutes	**Frequency:** Once	**Level of Difficulty:** Moderate

Instructions: Self-compassion researcher Dr. Kristin Neff defines self-compassion as having three components: **(1)** self-kindness, or avoiding harshly criticizing yourself; **(2)** recognizing your own humanity, or realizing that all individuals have flaws, experience pain, and possess imperfections, as this is what makes us human; and **(3)** mindfulness, or possessing a nonjudgmental, moment-to-moment awareness. Self-compassion is different from self-esteem, as the latter involves how much you view yourself to be valuable, whereas self-compassion involves accepting yourself even in times of difficulty or failure. Research shows those with high levels of self-compassion tend to be happier and more optimistic, which is good news for us all.

For millennials in particular, practicing self-compassion can be a true challenge. When everyone around you seems to always look picture perfect, or to be #slayingit, it can feel like you never measure up or that you need to keep working harder to achieve more. Self-compassion is more than just giving yourself a break or a trite compliment. It is about truly embracing yourself, with all your imperfections, the way you would a best friend. Think about all those times you lifted up a friend, negated their harsh self-criticisms, and reminded them that we all go through tough times but are worthy of happiness and love nonetheless. Now, turn that attitude toward yourself, and test your own level of self-compassion by answering the questions that follow.

How I Typically Act
Toward Myself in Difficult Times

Please read each statement carefully before answering. To the left of each item, indicate how often you behave in the stated manner, using the following scale:

Almost Never				Almost Always
1	2	3	4	5

_____ 1. When I fail at something important to me, I become consumed by feelings of inadequacy.

_____ 2. I try to be understanding and patient toward those aspects of my personality I don't like.

_____ 3. When something painful happens, I try to take a balanced view of the situation.

_____ 4. When I'm feeling down, I tend to feel like most other people are probably happier than I am.

_____ 5. I try to see my failings as part of the human condition.

_____ 6. When I'm going through a very hard time, I give myself the caring and tenderness I need.

_____ 7. When something upsets me, I try to keep my emotions in balance.

_____ 8. When I fail at something that's important to me, I tend to feel alone in my failure.

_____ 9. When I'm feeling down, I tend to obsess and fixate on everything that's wrong.

_____10. When I feel inadequate in some way, I try to remind myself that feelings of inadequacy are shared by most people.

_____11. I'm disapproving and judgmental about my own flaws and inadequacies.

_____12. I'm intolerant and impatient toward those aspects of my personality I don't like.

To obtain a total self-compassion score, reverse score the following items (1, 4, 8, 9, 11, 12), meaning (1 = 5, 2 = 4, 3 = 3, 4 = 2, 5 = 1) and compute the total. An "average" score would be in the middle, so out of a maximum 60 possible, this would equate with 30.

Raes, F., Pommier, E., Neff, K. D., & Van Gucht, D. (2011). Construction and factorial validation of a short form of the Self-Compassion Scale. *Clinical Psychology & Psychotherapy, 18*, 250–255.

While it is important not to get caught up in the details of scoring, this exercise can help alert you to the various aspects of self-compassion and how you might start working on integrating more of these practices into your own life. For example, two ways that you can actively practice self-compassion include journaling and self-care. Consider practicing the micro and macro self-care strategies discussed earlier in this workbook, as well as journaling. You can also write self-affirmations and post them in visible spaces as a means of reminding yourself of your worth and abilities. More information on developing self-compassion can be found in the Recommended Readings.

Finally, take some time to write down a few reflections and observations regarding your experience of taking this assessment:

_____

_____

_____

_____

_____

Raes, F., Pommier, E., Neff, K. D., & Van Gucht, D. (2011). Construction and factorial validation of a short form of the Self-Compassion Scale. *Clinical Psychology & Psychotherapy, 18*, 250–255.

Tool #25 | Five-Minute Mindful Cup Meditation

THERAPIST OVERVIEW

Perhaps one of the most accessible and relatable ways to introduce meditation involves the mindful tea, coffee, or beverage meditation. So many millennials quickly gulp down their coffee before (or even while) heading out the door that the simple ritual of savoring this beverage has been stripped down to nothing more than ingesting a drug that keeps them fueled and that allows them to tackle the many things thrown their way.

Whether it is afternoon high tea in England or an ancient Japanese tea ceremony, the act of savoring a warm and soothing beverage has historically been built into the day as the main event rather than the sideshow. Much time, care, and attention are paid to boiling water, steeping, and slowly ingesting a nourishing beverage, whether in ceremonies or at home. Encouraging millennials to take five minutes or less each day to slow down while they enjoy their morning beverage is a highly efficacious way of helping them build in mindful moments. Given that tea, coffee, lemon water, and other beverages are often consumed in the first few hours of the day, it is also an excellent way to start the day off with a nod toward mindfulness.

Furthermore, many millennials find themselves struggling with an afternoon slump that requires a "pick-me-up" to get them through the day, which provides them a second opportunity to practice this five-minute beverage meditation. Something as simple as an afternoon cup of tea enjoyed with a piece of dark chocolate can be a healthy indulgence when it is truly savored (Bush, 2015). While we can all be tempted to ever multitask and guzzle down our drinks while typing away furiously, it is a highly informative and important challenge for clients to integrate mindfulness into their lives.

In-Session Tip:
You can easily demonstrate this skill for your client in session, though this is certainly not necessary in order to introduce this practice. Many clinics and offices offer clients a cup of tea or coffee while they wait, and many therapists may coincidentally be sipping some peppermint or chamomile tea during the session themselves. Taking a quiet and mindful moment to drink a warm beverage together can truly bring this practice to life, and it can be informative to process this experience with the client as well. Was it "awkward" for them to sit silently until they finished their coffee? Did they get impatient or bored? Did they feel self-conscious? As many of these experiences closely mirror what they might experience during a typical seated meditation, experiencing and processing these reactions may help them later on as they tackle more challenging forms of mindfulness and meditation.

Five-Minute Mindful Cup Meditation

Duration: 5-10 minutes	**Frequency:** Daily	**Level of Difficulty:** Easy

Instructions: Learning to practice mindfulness is not nearly as complicated or esoteric as it might seem. In fact, you can easily start building your mindfulness toolkit by integrating small moments of mindfulness first thing in the morning. If you're like most millennials, there is a good chance you start your day with some type of warm beverage. Whether it is an almond milk lattè, matcha, lemon water, or tea, you may find yourself often chugging it (and possibly burning yourself!) as you head out the door. Or, you might sip on it throughout your morning commute, whether you are stuck in traffic or taking the subway into work. Learning to build in only a few minutes to truly savor and enjoy your morning cup can go a long way in capturing a peaceful moment to yourself before the hustle and bustle of the day begins.

If you have ever really timed yourself, then you might have learned that drinking a cup of any warm beverage doesn't really take that long at all. As long as it was not brewed to a boiling point that will burn your throat, even with a few minutes of cooling, it will likely take you less than five minutes to drink a cup of tea, coffee, or any other beverage of choice. Starting tomorrow, set a timer for five minutes and see if you can focus solely on the experience of drinking. No fancy meditations or mantras required. You can close your eyes the entire time or focus your gaze on the swirling steam raising from the cup. You might focus on the warmth radiating into your hands as you grasp your cup with both hands. Don't try to change or judge your thoughts or get too in your head about the experiment. Just focus on your drink.

In the event that you have more than five minutes and have been meaning to make time for another mindfulness activity, see if you can pair the two. Maybe you set your timer for 10 minutes and you journal for a few minutes as you drink, or after you drink. Or, you read an inspirational quote from a book, read scripture, or practice chanting a mantra. As you become more accustomed to this five-minute beverage period, you might find it easier to extend the time to include even more good-for-you behaviors.

Daily Mindful Commute Practice

THERAPIST OVERVIEW

Have you ever had the experience of driving while on autopilot? You get in your car, drive for 20 minutes, and—before you even realize it—reach your destination without any sense of what happened while you were driving. This is an all-too-common experience for many of us. But for multitasking millennials in particular, this can be an additionally hazardous experience, as many are checking and responding to emails and text messages while stopped at an intersection (or worse yet, while driving). Even though texting and driving is illegal in most states, especially in cities with plentiful traffic, the urge is still there for many millennials hoping to eke out a bit more work and maximize efficiency. Therefore, moving millennials from a place of mindlessness to mindfulness can be highly beneficial. Instead of getting angry, angsty, or impatient during their commute, they can learn to tap into practicing key mindfulness skills.

In order to help millennials start living in the moment instead of coasting by on autopilot, you can introduce them to the daily mindful commute. Discuss how this practice can help them enact the idea of moment-to-moment awareness that is a staple of mindfulness practice. Instead of getting lost in their thoughts, worries, or other concerns in their life, they can reconnect with their five senses and intentionally absorb what is going on around them. Rather than ruminate about getting that project done, they can go on a scavenger hunt of sorts during their commute, looking for new stimuli in their environment that they may not have previously noticed.

Often, focusing on nature is a readily accessible way to start out. Even if a client is residing in an urban area, there are often nearby parks, flowers in shop windows, or even Christmas tree lots they might be passing. Inducing the unique aspects of the changing seasons and nature is another helpful hint of what they might be looking for on their "hunt." As mindfulness can often feel unapproachable to clients, encouraging them to start with easily digestible practices, such as this one, can ideally help them to establish longer-term healthy habits.

Daily Mindful Commute Practice

Duration: 10-15 minutes	**Frequency:** Daily	**Level of Difficulty:** Easy

Instructions: Daily moments of mindfulness need not be fancy to be impactful. There are plentiful opportunities all throughout our day to practice mindfulness, and believe it or not, our commute is another simple place to implement these tools.

Many years ago, when I was an intern at Berkeley, I recall my epiphany when I stopped listening to my incessant stream of thoughts on my two mile walk to campus and instead started looking at all the sites around me instead. It turned out that I was missing out on the most gorgeous bush of flowers that I happened to walk by every day. I was even more impressed to later learn that they had the beautiful name of angel's trumpets. There were also all sorts of shops I hadn't realized were there, including a gelato store that later became a weekly staple.

It can be so easy to focus on getting from point A to point B that we miss everything that happens in between. It is natural to get caught up in our thoughts, or to simply avoid getting into a traffic accident. But every day is a new opportunity to truly take in what is happening around us. Tomorrow, during your commute, see if you can notice one or two new things that you may have missed when taking your regular route. Perhaps it is the leaves turning in the late summertime indicating the coming of fall, or even a street name that you never bothered to actually read on the sign. There are hundreds of tiny details we miss on a regular basis when we are on autopilot. See if you can even keep a journal or running list of the new things you discover each day on your way to work.

In the event that you work from home, maybe it is a daily walk you go on, or your route to get groceries, during which you can engage in this practice. The idea is to start paying attention and using your senses to really take in your daily experiences instead of being victim to your incessant stream of thoughts. Maybe you never noticed the smell of wafting donuts from a shop you drive past, or you never noticed that cacti can actually have blooms on them. Wherever you live and whatever your circumstances, you can allow yourself the opportunity to experience moments of nature in your daily commute.

To take an advanced step, consider changing up your route every now and again if you can. I used to live in an area where I could hop off the freeway and take suburban streets to work instead. This not only saved me time, but it also allowed me to take in sights, drive past a pretty park, and look at foliage in a way that would not have been possible on the freeway. If it is the holiday season, consider a detour to look at lights and décor. Building in time to pay attention to our surroundings is a key element of mindfulness.

Tool #27 | Daily Cleansing Rituals

THERAPIST OVERVIEW

In his best-selling book, *Wherever You Go, There You Are: Mindfulness Meditation in Every Day,* Dr. Jon Kabat-Zinn (1994) discusses a humorous anecdote on what happens when we let our minds wander without reigning them back in. He describes the common experience of bathing and thinking about a work meeting or other problem. He shares that when we let ourselves get lost in our thoughts, we've actually brought the meeting into the shower with us. Our bosses, the secretary, everyone. In the shower. With us. Enough said!

You can help millennials reign in their wandering mind through the use of "mini-meditations" (Tolle, 2004). In contrast to more formal mindful meditation practice, which involves sitting for extended periods of time while actively meditating, mini-meditations involve small acts of mindfulness that individuals can incorporate throughout the day. For example, waiting for the elevator to come is a moment to practice mindfulness, as is putting on our shoes, washing our hands, or washing the dishes. We can make each of these simple moments meditative by clearing our minds the best we can and just paying attention to our breathing and the task at hand.

Using the concept of mini-meditations, millennials can transform the daily process of cleansing and bathing from routine to ritual simply by paying attention. Again, as with the daily beverage and commute practices, these are simple ways to integrate mindfulness into everyday life without any extra effort required. The next time clients take a bath or shower, encourage them to fully focus on just that—bathing. The scents of soaps, the sensation of warmth, and the sounds of water. Learning to catch themselves when their minds drift can help them continue practicing mindfulness and can bring more awareness to their daily lives.

Daily Cleansing Ritual

Duration: 15-20 minutes	**Frequency:** Daily	**Level of Difficulty:** Easy

Instructions: Being a highly hygienic millennial, chances are you either shower or take a bath every day. In fact, you might even hoard fizzy bath bombs and special lotions. The next time you are bathing, see if you can use this as an opportunity to practice mindfulness. Seeing as how mindfulness in its essence involves focusing on breath and moment-to-moment awareness, all you have to do is simply pay attention. Have you ever forgotten if you've used shampoo or conditioned already? Or, have there been times when you couldn't remember if you washed your face? That's probably a good sign you were on autopilot and not really paying attention to what you were doing. A simple way to really focus on your bathing ritual is to bring your awareness to your five senses:

- **Smell**: Bring your awareness to the scents of your soaps, shampoos, and any other products you may use. You might even consider using a different scent to really awaken your senses with something new.

- **Touch**: Feel the warmth and pressure of the water on your skin. The sensation of a warm towel wrapping you up as you step onto a cushy bathmat. If there are areas where you can improve these sensations, such as using a fabric softener on your towels to keep them from being stiff and scratchy, do it! Or, buy that foam bathmat you can sink into.

- **Sound**: Listen to the sounds of the water, the tub draining, and even the water hitting the shower curtain or ground below.

- **Sight**: Really look at the suds of soap on your sponge or skin. If your hair is long enough to see the strands, really examine them. Pay attention to your skin and the look of steam in the shower. Take in any other countless details you may have been missing.

- **Taste**: Ideally, you aren't getting soap in your mouth, but if you do, what an opportunity to make an observation! You might also swish your mouth with the warm water from the shower.

As you become accustomed to paying more and more attention to the actual act of bathing, and you can spend more time focused on the experience itself rather than your thoughts, you might consider an advanced skill. Once a week or even once a month, draw yourself a bath and spend 45 minutes to an hour soaking, breathing, and meditating. As water can be deeply rejuvenating and replenishing, a bath can be an excellent way to hone your mindfulness practice.

You might find that, over time, you genuinely enjoy bathing as an escape from the chaos of daily life. Or, you may discover looking for small but impactful ways of enhancing the bathing experience. It can be incredible what a difference a new soap with an amazing smell can make, or how luxurious a new towel can feel. As an added bonus, these are all forms of self-care as well!

Tool #28 | Tech-Guided Meditation

THERAPIST OVERVIEW

Once millennials have gotten into the habit of engaging in small, daily mindfulness practices, many will be comfortable making the natural jump to more formal meditation practices. Using technology to guide meditations is a helpful way for them to start integrating small, dedicated periods of time to meditation.

There are numerous free and well-regarded tools available for clients to experiment with. Whether clients prefer using a desktop, their cell phone, or even a television, there are countless resources for them to try. YouTube is a very accessible and popular site that millennials use to look up everything from recipes to closet organization strategies. Clients can use various search terms and experiment with whatever speaks to them initially. For example, the concept of autonomous sensory meridian response (ASMR) gained much popularity on YouTube, with videos of women whispering about brushing hair to ease individuals into a peaceful and deep sleep. Clients will sometimes come in and discuss how they enjoy such videos and find them useful before the therapist even has a chance to recommend such tools.

Apps are another highly popular way to introduce clients to meditation—and many times, clients will report already having tried tools such as Headspace®, Calm®, and Insight Timer®. The latter is an app I recommend frequently to clients, as it features a global map of other people who are engaging in meditation at the very same time. Additionally, it can organize guided meditations based on the amount of time clients have available, and it offers meditations as short as zero to five minutes. There are no excuses why a client can't do a one-minute guided meditation this way!

While moving away from digital devices in the long term is ideal, it can sometimes be helpful to use technology to normalize how effective short periods of meditation can be. Further, guided meditations are much more accessible for beginners, as the quiet and solitude of a seated practice can bring up much frustration and discomfort, and can possibly be triggering for trauma survivors. Guided meditations can also be extremely helpful in that they actually *teach* the principles of mindfulness and meditation. Given that apps such as Insight Timer feature thousands of meditation instructors, there are countless ways for clients to approach this practice, and one teacher may resonate more with a client than another.

Another benefit of tech-guided meditations is that they easily allow clients to track the frequency, duration, and time spent in this pursuit. Millennials often get caught up in maintaining "streaks," such as in Snapchat, and many meditation apps also make a game of sorts in giving clients points or special accolades for regular daily practice. While this is certainly an extrinsic motivator, it can help give reticent clients a boost until their motivation becomes more intrinsically based over time.

Finally, a major benefit of tech-guided meditations is that they can take pressure off of the therapist during an intake or crisis session. Many times, the full therapy hour can be spent discussing the details of a concern or getting to know a client for the first time. This can leave little time for a calming intervention, such as a meditation, in session. While it can be beneficial to sit with clients in silence during the session, when there is little to no time, you can easily recommend tech-guided apps that clients can integrate into their daily lives outside of session. At the same time, with the availability of many one-minute guided meditations, it may sometimes be appropriate to leave time for a quick meditation at the end of session.

Tech-Guided Meditation

Duration: 15-20 minutes	**Frequency:** Daily	**Level of Difficulty:** Easy

Instructions: For many millennials, the idea of any type of meditation can invoke a host of emotions. Some are intrigued, others are immediately uninterested. Meditation is sometimes associated with images of Buddhist temples, chanting, and incense, while others may associate it with the one time they visited their friendly neighborhood yoga studio. Whatever your background and experience, a simple way to learn (or re-integrate) meditation into your life can involve the use of your trusty daily companion: your smartphone.

Meditation apps abound, and different tools intrigue different folks. Instead of "assigning" you one particular meditation app over another, run a search, download several, and see what you liked and didn't like. But be sure to really give it a fair chance. Finding a guided meditation you like can take *lots* of practice and time. It's important to use different search terms, try various instructors, and vary the times of day you engage in this practice. For example, some people might find that their anxiety is highest first thing in the morning but try out the meditation app late at night instead. Finding an optimal time for meditation takes some trial and error. Fortunately, since there are guided meditations that take no more than five minutes, it can help to break up your meditation time into various periods. For example, you might aim for 15 minutes of meditation per day and break it up by practicing five minutes in the morning, at lunchtime, and before bed.

Here, list the name of two or three guided meditation apps you'd like to try:

_____

_____

_____

Then, schedule it! Have a reminder pop up on your phone or computer. Or, write it in a paper planner. Write out your plan for integrating guided meditation here:

_____

_____

_____

_____

Finally, after a week of integrating these tools, write down any reflections, insights, or other pertinent information regarding this experiment:

_____

_____

_____

_____

Tool #29 | Japanese Forest Bathing

THERAPIST OVERVIEW

For millennials whose minds are often distracted and buzzing with thoughts and concerns, slowing down enough to meditate can be a challenge. While the goal throughout this book has been to slowly but surely introduce moments of mindfulness to make way for periods of more concentrated, seated meditation, a walking meditation very much accomplishes this same goal. The practice of walking meditation involves taking a slow and deliberate walk in which the focus of your attention is on the act of walking itself. You are mindful of each and every footstep as your legs rise and fall with each step—from the sensation of your heel lifting off the ground, to the ball of your foot holding the weight of your body.

Although walking meditation can be a beautiful practice, it can run the risk of being painfully slow for many fast-paced millennials. Focusing on every single footstep can easily cause frustration, and frankly boredom, in this practice. Therefore, for many millennials, it may be more appropriate to start out with the concept of forest bathing, or *Shinrin-yoku* as the Japanese call it, which has been gaining popularity in recent years. As opposed to a walking meditation, which millennials can do in their neighborhood or even backyard, forest bathing relies heavily on immersing oneself with nature to cleanse and heal. It involves seeking out a natural area, ideally with forest cover if possible, and taking a slow, meditative walk while deeply breathing in the fresh forest air. Hiking, tending to plants, and general appreciation for nature is on the rise among millennials, so many clients may favor forest bathing as an eventual springboard to more a more formal walking meditation practice. Further, while many walking meditations focus on the intricacies of one's footfall and move at a very slow pace, forest bathing can take the form of a slow-paced hike toward which clients might be more naturally inclined.

In-Session Tip:
Throughout my therapy practice, I have often been fortunate to work in locations near natural areas. Whether on a college campus or in a suburban area, there has typically been a park or nature trail within short walking distance of my office. It has not been uncommon for me to go with clients on a nature walk during the session. While, of course, you must assess client comfort with this (given confidentiality, especially in small towns and on college campuses) and safety (particularly with minors), the benefits of getting out of the office and into nature are a phenomenal form of in-vivo skill practice. In fact, many parents have been thrilled when I have asked their permission to take a teen on a short walk near the office. They get fresh air (as do I!) and some healthy, gentle exercise. Just be sure to stash some tennis shoes in your office for these excursions.

Japanese Forest Bathing

| **Duration:** 20-40 minutes | **Frequency:** Weekly/Monthly | **Level of Difficulty:** Moderate |

Instructions: Stepping outside to get some fresh air is one of the quickest boosts to mood if you have been indoors all day. Even in the snowiest and wettest conditions, taking a few deep breaths of fresh air can rejuvenate and enliven you. There is even a type of nature therapy called *Shinrin-yoku*, which is the Japanese term used to describe forest bathing. Developed in the 1980s, it refers to a peaceful, deeply healing, and preventative health practice that involves taking a meditative walk under a forest canopy. While there are some specialized forest therapy programs, the general elements of forest bathing involve bringing your awareness to your senses in the present moment as you immerse yourself in the natural environment, breathe the fresh air, slow down, and let your mind refocus. Several groups of researchers (Hansen et al., 2017) across the globe have found that taking a mindful walk in nature can bring a host of benefits, including:

- Increased positive emotions
- Decreased blood pressure
- Decreased stress
- Increased immune functioning
- Increased focus and attention
- Increased energy
- Improved sleep

Not bad at all for time spent communing with nature! Of course, our busy lives can prevent us from taking such time for contemplation and intentionality. However, making the time even once a month (weather permitting) to visit a forest and spending some time there can be deeply healing. While it is helpful to find some place relatively peaceful and quiet, it is important to ensure your safety, so you might consider bringing along a friend or partner. If being outdoors in the woods is not easily accessible for you, then simply go outside in your neighborhood. Practice experiencing your neighborhood with a *beginner's mind*—where you see, listen, and walk around your neighborhood with fresh eyes and ears, experiencing it as if for the first time.

During your walk, consider using the following guide to help you focus on the sensations of the forest and escape the constant stream of thoughts you might typically experience:

- **Sight:** Observe all the minutiae of the forest environment, from the tiniest twigs to large, powerful tree trunks that have been there for over a century.

- **Sound:** Listen for the crackle of every twig breaking and sound of every leaf crunching. Listen for the sounds of the wind sweeping through the trees. Birds may chirp, and squirrels may chase each other. Hear the forest's unique symphony.

- **Smell:** One of the most instantaneous ways we are transported to another time and place is through our sense of smell. Olfactory memories can be powerful, so make some new ones at the forest. Take in the woodsy scent, the smell of pine, cedar, or whatever type of foliage you are experiencing.

- **Touch:** As you walk through the forest, allow your fingers to graze gently past branches and tree trunks. Feel the rough ridges and the soft moss. Ground down through your feet and feel the undulations of the forest trails and path, each foot gently stepping ahead of the other, supported by nature.

- **Taste:** There is nothing quite like forest air. Take many slow deep breaths, filling your lungs and body with cleansing air.

After your excursion, consider bringing the forest home. There are many ways to re-create the experience of nature in your own home. Perhaps you buy a few small indoor plants and water them regularly. You might notice that each time you water the soil, you get the distinct aroma of nature (and lawn care stores!). You might light a scented candle that has a woodsy scent to it or listen to the sounds of nature using a sound machine or your phone. There are many creative ways to bring the soothing calm of nature into your everyday life. List some ideas for ways you might bring nature into your life using the five senses:

Sight: _____

_____

Sound: _____

_____

Smell: _____

_____

Touch: _____

_____

Taste: _____

_____

Finally, for an even more advanced practice, see if you can find a local Japanese or Chinese garden in an area near you. Or, maybe you find a Zen garden or church labyrinth. These are incredible opportunities to practice walking meditation on an advanced level. Given that the norm in these gardens is to linger, slow down, and take one's time, no one will be looking at you strangely. It is *expected* you walk at a snail's pace! So consider a true meditative walk in a designated area near you.

Seated Meditation

Tool #30

THERAPIST OVERVIEW

Perhaps one of the most classic meditations, which many beginners are familiar with, is the basic seated meditation. Given its simplicity and accessibility, it can prove to be an easily demonstrable skill within the therapy session. Psychologist and mindfulness expert Dr. Thomas Bien (2006) shares that for therapists whose primary theoretical orientation is mindfulness, it can be appropriate, after an initial explanation and disclaimer, to start or end each and every therapy session with a brief meditation.

Regularly practicing meditation with clients in session is a powerful way to make time and space for quiet sitting, as well as to show how easily accessible this practice can be. Furthermore, many clients come to actively look forward to these few moments each week in therapy and may even report this is the only time they really sit in silence. Millennials are constantly bombarded by the sounds of their busy world, whether it be the ping of a new text message, the sounds of the keyboard clacking under their fingers, or a notification on their phone signaling a new "like" on their social media page. Taking time to make space for stillness is key in helping them slow down. While it can be uncomfortable or seem unnatural to start and end sessions with meditation, it is certainly worth experimenting with in your clinical practice.

However, I recommend testing out this approach with perhaps a small handful of clients on your caseload first instead of making it a one-size-fits-all mandatory meditation for all. As many therapists are aware, for clients who have trauma histories, meditation can initially be contraindicated and highly triggering. Therefore, unless trauma is your specialty and you possess training and expertise in working with trauma survivors, insisting on a seated meditation may not be the wisest course of action. That being said, as a therapist, you will quickly come to recognize which clients are more receptive than others to meditation and how to integrate and normalize this into your practice.

Another factor to note is timing, as well as the particular clients who are most ideally suited for a simple seated meditation in session. For example, I have worked with millennials who come into session and start talking a mile a minute, hardly stopping for breath. These clients are so accustomed to living each and every day in this manner, and the therapy process can be instrumental in disrupting this harmful pattern. Demonstrating how to slow down in session with these clients can help create lifelong change. On the flip side, I have also worked with clients resistant to the therapy process altogether. For these clients, a seated meditation might be one of the worst interventions I could come up with. Pay attention to client match when it comes to this approach.

In the exercise that follows, instructions for a simple seated meditation are provided. There are countless ways to do a seated meditation, so instead of providing a strict "script," I have suggested particular aspects of this practice that you might integrate into your sessions. Feel free to experiment with the instructions and stylistic points provided.

In-Session Tip:

When introducing clients to a basic seated meditation, teaching them about diaphragmatic breathing can also help. I typically describe this as belly breathing, evoking the image of a baby sleeping in a crib. It is usually their little belly that rises and falls as they sleep on their back, as this is the most natural and fullest expression of breathing. When we are anxious, we breathe short, shallow breaths from the chest instead of taking long, slow breaths from the abdomen. To demonstrate diaphragmatic breathing, I use these three steps:

1. I ask clients to put one hand on their chest and one on their abdomen to see if they can focus on having the hand on their abdomen rise and fall with each breath, instead of the one on their chest;

2. I ask them to put both hands on their abdomen and have them imagine a balloon filling and emptying, with their fingers breaking apart across the belly when they inhale fully and coming back together again when they exhale; and

3. I encourage them to place a small book on their belly while lying down at home (I never do this in session to avoid discomfort) and to watch it rise and fall as they breathe. When doing these exercises, I encourage clients to breathe in and out through their nose the entire time without changing their breathing pattern too drastically or causing any struggle.

Seated Meditation

Duration: 5-20 minutes	**Frequency:** Weekly	**Level of Difficulty:** Moderate

Instructions: A simple seated meditation is one of the most basic and accessible types of practice available. An often-surprising fact for many individuals is that the entire purpose of yoga at its inception was to prepare the body for long and intensive periods of seated meditation practice. Whether it is through hip opening or cleansing and purifying the body prior to a seated practice, it all comes down to sitting with the breath.

While it may not sound exceptionally special or difficult (except for the part about keeping one's thoughts at bay), seated meditation has transformational powers. Research indicates meditation has the ability to help with anxiety, depression, and pain, and it can even result in brain changes among the most experienced practitioners (Fox et al., 2014; Goyal et al., 2014). While not enough is known to see the long-term impact of this practice, the available evidence suggests meditation can change your brain for the better! While there are various meditation scripts available, not every script will resonate with every person, so I've instead provided some simple tips to help you integrate a seated meditation practice into your routine.

• Start small: Set a timer, and start with 1 minute. As you become comfortable, increase the timer to 2 minutes, 5 minutes, 10 minutes, 15 minutes, and beyond.

• Sit down on a cushion, chair, yoga mat, or any other surface that allows your back to sit upright. Your legs can be crossed or folded. You can sit on your heels or with your feet out in front of you. While your posture should ideally be erect, do not strain or over-articulate the motion either. A common image is to sit like a mountain: firm, grounded, and strong.

• Your hands can go anywhere. Folded in your lap. Upright on your knees or upper thighs with your palms facing up. Or, palms grounding down on your legs or even the ground beneath you. You can hold a mudra if that is comfortable and familiar to you (e.g., thumb and middle finger touching), but don't sweat it! There are no right or wrong hand positions, but resist the urge to fidget the best you can.

• Breathe in through the nostrils and out through the nostrils. That's it! Don't try to change your breathing by elongating the in-breath or out-breath. Over time, you might come to observe that taking long, slow exhales is incredibly calming, but you don't need to worry about altering the breath in complicated ways.

- Close your eyes. Or, look at a stationary point with your lids lowered.

- Turn on soft music or a noise machine if it helps, but the room can be perfectly quiet or there can be ambient noise in the background.

- The use of essential oils, crystals, or whatever else gets you in the right frame of mind is completely optional. It's all about setting up your environment for success.

- Clear your mind as best you can, but don't force it. Focus on your breath and the sensation of air entering and exiting your nostrils.

- If you find that thoughts keep coming up, you can count the breath to give your mind something to do. With each exhale, count to 10 and once you reach 10, start back at 1. If you find that your mind still wanders, and you can't remember where you were, no problem. There is a simple solution: Start back at 1.

- If focusing on your nostrils and breath isn't working (and counting the breath isn't either), start acknowledging your thoughts. You can use some imagery to help: Imagine that your thoughts are clouds passing through a beautiful and clear blue sky, or that your thoughts are leaves floating down a river. You can also imagine your thoughts are tucked away safely in a hot air balloon that is floating far, far away.

As you become increasingly comfortable with this basic seated practice, you can switch things up as often as you'd like. You might try out burning incense one time or see what it's like to sit in a new posture. You might turn off the music in the background for total silence. If you observe or start to find just the right recipe for your own personal seated meditation practice, note some key steps here:

_____

_____

_____

_____

Yog-ahhh: Preparation

THERAPIST OVERVIEW

It is worth beginning this section by saying that encapsulating the thousands of years of yogic wisdom in a single activity will never do it justice. However, given the incredible healing power of yoga, it cannot go unmentioned. Not only does it have profound physical benefits in terms of weight loss and cardiovascular health, but it also improves memory, attention, concentration, and sleep. It has also been found to reduce stress, increase self-acceptance, and enhance overall mood (Lamb, 2004). Yoga, it seems, is remarkable for our psychological, physical, and cognitive well-being.

Yoga continues to rise in popular culture with the meteoric rise of clothing manufacturers that have marketed yoga attire as normative, everyday clothing. In turn, millennials are very aware of yoga, and many have likely tried a class at some point throughout their lives. However, the popularity of the practice has also in some ways altered its origins. Many former aerobics and Pilates instructors now teach yoga without any formal training in the practice. Others fuse yoga with intense core workouts and boast "power" yoga classes that will make you break a sweat. And for those who really enjoying getting drenched or working out in sweltering conditions, there is the option of Bikram or "hot" yoga, which is conducted in rooms with temperatures around 100 degrees Fahrenheit and around 40% humidity.

For many millennials, these types of classes may represent exactly what they are looking for in a yoga practice. But for yoga to be therapeutic or otherwise beneficial, such intensity is hardly needed. In the following handout, some basic preparatory psychoeducation is provided for clients who are new to the practice or who are looking to get back into it.

Yog-ahhh: Preparation

Duration: 10-15 minute (reading)	**Frequency:** Once	**Level of Difficulty:** Easy

Instructions: Whether you are a yoga newbie, an advanced practitioner, or your only experience with yoga involves wearing yoga pants, there are many factors to take into consideration when establishing a yoga routine. From physical safety to therapeutic benefits, it is important to be aware of the various types of yoga that can help you, as well as general tips for finding success in picking a class. This handout outlines six steps for you to consider when finding the right type of yoga fit for you.

Six Steps to Finding the Right Yoga Class for You

1. Be kind

The idea of exhibiting self-compassion and kindness toward our entire self and body is one that we struggle with globally. Many times, we are too harsh and critical of ourselves, and this seeps into other areas of our lives. For example, I've often had clients discuss the idea of starting a yoga practice. After years of being inactive, they select the most physically challenging class and are quick to judge themselves when they fall short of their own expectations. So pick a class that fits your needs, and adjust accordingly. I've most often appreciated yoga instructors that truly cater to the needs of beginners. Though many will say they allow beginners into their classes, I've seen students unfamiliar with terminology and poses struggle and never return to classes. So even if your instructor doesn't say certain poses are optional, or that you may take a break, allow yourself to rest between poses if needed. There is no need to struggle.

2. Start slow

Know that it's okay to begin with something "easy." The best yoga class I ever took was freshman year of college. It was called "gentle yoga fitness" and was co-sponsored with a local senior citizen's center. It was slow, gentle, and one of the most relaxing yoga classes I've ever taken. Inhales and exhales were expertly coordinated with every one of our yoga poses so we could actually see the improvement each time we came in and out of a pose. Each time, we stretched just a tiny bit further and deeper, and it was amazing to see the improvement in just a few breaths. Therefore, more meditative and breath-centered yoga practices could be ideal for beginners. After all, the goal may not be a total body workout per se; it may be something much simpler, such as relaxation or light stretching.

3. Pick a small class

Though community classes are typically the most financially accessible, they are usually the most packed as well. For starters, look up the background of your yoga instructor online to learn more about their training, and if possible, pick a small class. This can lead to more one-on-one instruction, as well as poses tailored to meet your needs. Good yoga instructors will often ask if you have any physical restrictions or have any requests, and they will take the time to adjust your pose to keep you from injuring yourself.

Having been in larger classes crammed with students, I've often found two common themes: (1) instructors don't always have the time (or space) to walk around and adjust each student individually, and (2) instructors don't always offer modifications to make the pose more or less challenging depending upon the student's level. For example, many poses can be made less strenuous by enlisting a wall as a stable agent to help with balance. I've often found that in larger classes, many students have some experience with yoga, so the challenge level is bumped up many more notches than a beginner would appreciate.

4. Props are fun!

Some of the best yoga classes I've taken have made innovative and effective use of a number of props: yoga blocks, blankets, and straps. In one fun class, they had us lay down in corpse pose with our body weight supported by only a few blocks, which made us feel like we were floating. Other times, blankets may be used to apply gentle pressure to open up tight areas, or blankets may be rolled up into logs to help open up the shoulders. These poses are sometimes the most therapeutic, as they encourage the gentle opening and relaxing of body parts. Many times, a series of poses may open up regions that traditionally hold tension, such as the shoulders and back. After doing these poses in succession, your body may hold little hope of storing tension there by the end of class.

5. Play the field, or rather the studio

Don't be afraid to try different classes, studios, and instructors. Shop around until you find something that fits your needs. Every time I move to a new area, I struggle to find yoga classes quite like the ones I took nearly a decade ago. These days, every studio I walk into seems to be power and core-driven. However, that is not to say more meditative and breath-centered studios do not exist. Also, don't be shy about approaching instructors frankly with questions and concerns. My favorite instructors are those who have emphasized yoga as the one place where you are not competing against anyone, including yourself. Ideally, a yoga instructor will challenge you but will also not push you to go further than you are comfortable. Some instructors include poses such as a shoulder stand as standard practice, while others consider it a more advanced pose. Figuring out the type of instructor and studio that works for you is essential. And of course, word of mouth is a great way to find good classes as well.

6. Think of yoga as play

Unlike a kickboxing class, yoga can really be fun and playful. Bring a buddy and make it a yoga date. One of my good friends and I once tried a Friday night candlelight yoga class that brought on bouts of giggles but was also a good workout. Certainly for the unaccustomed, many aspects of yoga may seem downright strange. The first time I ever had to inhale cat and exhale dog, my exhale came out as a burst of laughter. I have been to classes with chanting and with interesting nostril-sealing breath techniques. I've also nearly suffocated from the strong scent of incense in other classes. In the end, it challenges you to step outside of your comfort zone and to try something new. For some, yoga may be deeply spiritual, while for others it may be part of their regimen to obtain washboard abs.

Therapeutically, I have seen the benefits reaped by my clients who practice yoga while in therapy. For some, life circumstances have made it so that their former practice has dropped to the wayside, and for others it is a new experience entirely. I have known some yoga instructors to ask students to set aside an intention for each practice. Others have read spiritual or inspiring passages and quotes prior to the final resting posture. At times, I have thought these instructors are providing to students much of what therapists hope to give to clients—peace, awareness, self-compassion, contentment, and balance.

Previously published in *Psychology Today* by Bocci (2012)

Tool #32 | Yog-ahhh: Practice

THERAPIST OVERVIEW

The primary challenge in introducing yoga as a clinical recommendation is the breadth of practices and practitioners available. Many years ago, after receiving my own 200-hour yoga certification training, I began a yoga therapy group for teenage girls with anxiety. The practices were all restorative and highly adaptive for all body types. In fact, the overwhelming majority of my groups reported never having been physically active or even feeling comfortable being active due to their bodies and sense of shame. Therefore, while the group's main focus was anxiety relief through slow, restorative poses, the impacts were multitudinous and included improvements in self-image and body appreciation as well.

Unfortunately, many clients unknowingly walk into a heated Bikram studio, nearly faint, and never return to yoga again. Meanwhile, others who are intense athletes walk into a gentle yoga class, feel frustrated, and walk out. There is quite a bit of matching that must be done to fit client temperament with yogic style in order for clients to have an optimal experience. That being said, it is an undue burden for therapists to be aware of every available type of yoga, studio, or teacher nearby. Instead, the handout that follows presents basic information regarding several primary types of yoga, as well as some instructions that describe how clients can ease into a yoga practice that supports their therapy journey.

In-Session Tip:
While it is important to be mindful of not overstepping one's boundaries as a trained and certified practitioner of mental health versus yoga, it is not uncommon for therapists who practice yoga at home to bring this into the therapy room. In fact, there are already a number of workbooks and tools available for clinicians that explain how to integrate gentle elements of yoga into their work with clients. Of course, you should refrain from trying anything that might be overly strenuous or out of your area of expertise, as this can be a liability and cause possible injury to a client. However, if you happen to have your own home or studio practice—and you are comfortable leading a client in a simple stretch (e.g., forward fold with knees bent, upward stretch toward the sky coordinated with breath, simple seated twist or gentle side stretches)—then consider doing so with your millennial client. They may already be quite open and eager to practice these skills in session and may become motivated to do more at home or in a studio.

<u>client handout</u>

Yog-ahhh: Practice

Duration: 30-90 minutes   **Frequency:** Weekly   **Level of Difficulty:** Challenging

Instructions: The range of yoga styles available—and their accompanying esoteric lexicon (chakras, asanas, pranayama)—have had the unfortunate effect of scaring many people away from a practice that could markedly improve their overall health and quality of life. Certainly, if health concerns are present, you should consult with a physician prior to beginning any practice. However, if you feel ready to integrate some existing modalities into your current practice, here is a list of several of the most popular types of yoga to consider. Challenge yourself to try one or two types of each over the next several months. Perhaps you go to two classes a month with different instructors, with different modalities, or at different studios. Take advantage of the new student specials that often offer free or deeply discounted classes to try out.

Hatha

Hatha yoga is often described as a more "gentle yoga" that includes more basic levels of the practice. This type of yoga is often recommended for beginners, as classes move more slowly and teachers typically provide more cues for proper alignment. Postures are slow to get into, and there might be some muscular trembles as you hold a pose for four to five breaths, but you are gentle in coming out of the pose.

Vinyasa

Power yoga, core yoga, and other more intensive classes are often under the Vinyasa category. Vinyasa refers to a flow, so be prepared to move. Often, you alternate up and down on the mat (so watch out for dizziness). While you might move into challenging poses, there is often little to no "holding" of the pose as you quickly transition out.

Restorative

An ideal type of yoga for anxious types and novices, restorative yoga—like the name suggests—is focused on restoring and rejuvenating poses. Typically, these classes make use of plentiful props, pillows, blankets, and bolsters, and only four or five poses may be done in an entire class. This part often takes practitioners by surprise, but in restorative yoga, it is typically about relaxing into a supported pose that is held for long periods of time, often five to ten minutes or more. Generally, the goal of these classes is less about fitness and building muscles, and more about restoring peace of mind, equanimity, and deep relaxation. *Yoga nidra* is yoga that helps with sleep and can often include restorative postures to aid rest.

Yin

Similar to restorative yoga in terms of holding postures for long periods of time, yin yoga does not always feature a tremendous number of poses and can be a slower-paced class. Having said that, these classes can sometimes be more grueling and challenging than anticipated. For example, imagine you struggle with touching your toes—in a yin class, you might be in a forward bend pose for a full five minutes and might cramp up coming out of the pose, as yin does not feature the level of propping that restorative yoga does. But for many athletes, yin can be a perfect complement to their training due to the deep stretching and relaxation of muscles.

Iyengar

Named for its founder B. K. Iyengar, this type of yoga is very focused on alignment. This can be excellent for building a strong foundation, but it can also be intimidating for people who want to get lost in a crowd. Since proper alignment and form is so important in Iyengar yoga, expect a lot of adjustment from the teacher. While all forms of yoga can include adjustments—and you can always opt out—this type of yoga may involve more perfecting of poses than a beginner would like. On the flip side, Iyengar yoga teaches precision in a way that many yoga classes can neglect, leading to misalignment and injury later on down the road.

Bikram/Heated

Too often, people associate yoga with heated classes, even though this represents only a small portion of the types of yoga available. At the same time, heated yoga is popular because it offers a more grueling challenge. While some people equate Bikram and heated yoga as one and the same, there are some key differences between the two. For starters, Bikram gets up to 104 degrees, whereas heated yoga can be as low as 80 degrees. Bikram also features 26 core poses and lasts 90 minutes, and it's essentially more "hardcore" and strict, as talking is not permitted and floors are carpeted. In heated yoga, you can use candlelight, wooden floors, and have shorter class lengths. Caution is always recommended in these classes as there have been links to dangerously high core temperature, overstretching (which can lead to injury), and nausea and dizziness. Generally speaking, heated classes should not be a first pick for beginners or for therapeutic purposes.

Ashtanga/Mysore

Ashtanga is a major type of yoga developed by Sri K. Pattabhi Jois in his institute located in Mysore, India. One of the much more advanced forms of yoga, Ashtanga yoga is often taught in what is called the Mysore style. The form of yoga itself features a very specific sequence of sun salutations and poses that follow. Beginner Ashtanga classes can be led by an instructor, which helps students learn the specific poses and the sequencing. In contrast, Mysore involves students in a class all doing the poses at their own pace with additional assistance from the instructor as needed. Therefore, if you are a beginner, do *not* enter a Mysore class right off the bat. There is a good chance you won't know the poses or the structure, and will feel completely lost and out of place. Not the best way to start your yoga journey. Talking to a studio owner or assistant can help you identify what type of classes to take if you are interested in trying out this form of yoga.

Kundalini

Often referred to as one of the more spiritual branches of yoga, this type of practice often involves quick breaths and "snapping" of the belly back and forth in an effort to bring energy into the body. Kundalini yogis often discuss the idea of awakening the "shakti" or energy at the base of the spine through their poses. There is often chanting, mantras, and other spiritual elements in this practice. For open-minded millennials willing to try something completely new and different, this type of yoga is certainly recommended.

Aerial

One of the more adventurous types of yoga, aerial yoga often looks like what you might see professionals do at a circus. Aerial yoga is definitely not for beginners, although beginning classes do exist. Be prepared to be upside down and to support your entire weight in long silky curtains that are tethered to the ceiling. Aerial yoga is certainly ethereal and beautiful, and it can definitely be what some millennials are looking for. Just be mindful of safety and experience levels required.

Acro/Partner

Similar to aerial yoga, acro yoga is a more acrobatic form of yoga that is sometimes (although not exclusively) paired with partner yoga. For millennials looking to laugh and connect with a best friend or partner, this can definitely be a way to do so. Given this type of yoga features more "stunts," it should go without saying that this is not beginner's yoga. But should you already have a solid foundation when it comes fitness, this can be a fantastic and fun way to practice yoga and build community. Poses include postures that bring you up close and personal to your partner, as well as poses that literally bring you close to flying.

Tool #33	Accessing Wise Mind

THERAPIST OVERVIEW

The concept of wise mind is a powerful one that resonates easily with many millennials. The battle between head and heart—whether it is deciding on a job, a relationship, or another major life transition—often stumps many of our therapy clients. While their logical brain understands how to weigh pros and cons, their heart may be steering them in a completely different direction.

The issue of wise mind often comes up when millennials feel uncertain regarding their romantic relationships in particular. Their heart may flutter when their boyfriend sends them flowers at work or surprises them with a fancy dinner. But at the same time, they logically understand that he does not have the best track record. Maybe he has been unfaithful to past partners, has been divorced multiple times, or has a daughter whom they do not feel prepared to handle. Head and heart are in battle, and clients can drive themselves up the wall trying to determine the best course of action. Here is where wise mind comes into play. By gently guiding clients to a place of wise mind when they feel stuck, they can come to a place of deep knowing, one guided by their intuition, that helps get them unstuck.

As a therapist, you can make use of all the meditation and mindfulness skills you have been teaching your client thus far to help them start moving toward wise mind. This is the place of balance between head and heart that is best accessed through deep relaxation, peace, and equanimity. It is the space we engender when we come out of a meditation, prayer, restorative yoga practice, or forest walk. While accessing wise mind certainly isn't easy, most millennials can intuitively appreciate and understand that there is a third option beyond listening to their emotions or logical brain in making a decision. Wise mind is essentially a form of listening to their gut and intuition and becoming curious about what their wise mind is saying in a nonjudgmental, open manner. Ultimately, wise mind rests in the delicate intersection between our rational minds and our hearts.

Millennial Vignette

I have worked with many millennial college students nearing graduation and next big steps. I recall working with a talented and highly intelligent young woman who had dated the same kind and loving man the entirety of college. She was headed off to law school and he was headed off to med school, both on opposite coasts. He was willing to do long-distance, and she was torn inside. Would she ever meet someone she connected so strongly with again? But what if staying in the relationship meant she would shortchange herself the opportunity for new relationships with men who may be an even better match? Or would she let him go and regret the decision forever? This client was stuck in her head while trying to honor her heart. The concept of wise mind was a comforting one that allowed her to listen to her intuition, which she had been denying. She was so insistent on how the relationship made logical sense that she was forgoing listening to the part of her that wanted to let go. We discussed how to slowly remove herself from this relationship in a way that honored both of their feelings and needs.

Accessing Wise Mind

Duration: 15-20 minutes	**Frequency:** As Needed	**Level of Difficulty:** Challenging

Instructions: Have you ever found yourself stuck trying to make a decision, caught between your head and your heart? Maybe it was deciding on a new job or moving away from home for the first time. It can be agonizing as we write out "pros and cons" lists or simply feel nagged relentlessly by our emotions. This is where the concept of wise mind comes in. Our wise mind is in essence our intuition, our "gut" feeling. There might be a level of emotion involved in justifying a decision and a level of logic as well. But something deeper and more powerful overtakes us. Imagine this scenario:

You are on a walk in the middle of a nature trail on a beautiful day. The sun is shining down on the trees and flowers, and you are energized and feeling completely content. Then, you come across an injured bird whose wing appears broken. Meanwhile, you notice a small fox making its way toward its new prey. Without thinking, you jump into action. You untie the sweatshirt that was around your waist, scoop up the bird inside, and start quickly making your way away from the fox and toward your car parked at the trailhead.

In this scenario, you clearly did not have a well-thought-out plan in mind. You weren't thinking of vets you knew or even of what would happen if the fox started to attack you. You saw a living creature in need (emotions) and took action by rescuing it in your arms so the fox couldn't get to it (logic). Your wise mind was what helped you to merge the two seamlessly and instantaneously, allowing you to go with your gut rather than thinking about how expensive or difficult finding a vet might be (logic), or worrying about what would happen if you left the bird to become the fox's prey (emotions). The concept of wise mind is portrayed in the following diagram.

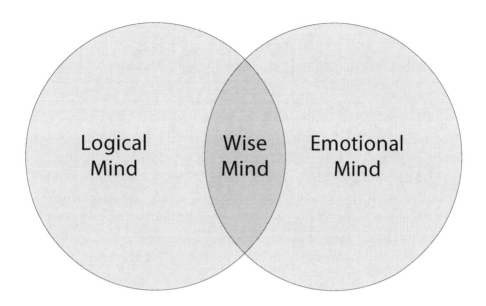

Logical Mind

Wise Mind

Emotional Mind

You might be thinking, this sounds great and all in theory, but how do I *access* my wise mind? Although it may seem simplistic, wise mind is most easily accessed in times of stillness that involve deep breathing from the belly while practicing mindfulness. Throughout this workbook, you have been given a plethora of different tools and strategies to help you increase your mindfulness skills. Some will stand out and really hit home, and others may feel too unrelatable. That's okay. As long as you find something that works, you can start accessing your wise mind through mindfulness practices.

Anytime you have had to make a major decision, you likely haven't made it without careful consideration. You likely thought it over, went to sleep, ruminated, and continued to think about it at the gym, during lunch, and so forth. Perhaps you even prayed about it in a place of worship. Point being, big decisions are made over time and are best made when not rushed. They can be even better and more fulfilling when they're made from a place of ease and equanimity. The next time you have a major decision to make, consider taking five minutes at a time just to breathe and empty your mind. (I know, it's harder than it sounds!) Consider journaling any immediate thoughts that come to mind afterward. Over time, you will become more and more skilled at accessing and practicing your wise mind.

THERAPIST OVERVIEW

For millennials who are not aware of how to manage their emotions in a safe manner, learning emotion regulation skills can be eye-opening to say the least. Having grown up during an era that normalized risky sexual behaviors and binge drinking, many millennials do not deal with challenging situations in a healthy manner. Far too many pop culture images exist of women blowing off steam through a night of heavy drinking with girlfriends and men hitting up bars or punching bags to get out anger. How many times have we seen images of morning hangovers and evidence of deeply regretted hookups?

When a client exhibits difficulty with emotion regulation, this is typically a sign that they are over-relying on emotional reasoning and under-relying on rational thinking. When a difficult situation occurs, such as being let go from a job, they are quick to jump to anger, hatred, self-loathing, fear, and a whole host of other emotions. Instead of sitting down and trying to access their wise mind, they are inclined to let their emotional mind run the show, which propels them into behaviors that actually exacerbate the problem. It is not that millennials are consciously (or even subconsciously) trying to punish themselves, but they often truly lack alternative coping skills. Allowing them to honor their feelings in a safe way, instead of trying to escape or numb themselves, is an important skill to learn. Additionally, it can help them build up their emotional resiliency and reduce their vulnerability to further problems down the line.

The **PLEASE MASTER** acronym is a helpful tool that can help millennials stay out of emotional mind and remain centered in a place of wise mind (Linehan, 2015). This tool emphasizes some key elements of well-being including: treating and managing **P**hysica**L** illnesses, **E**ating properly, **A**voiding mood altering substances (including alcohol and cannabis products), **S**leeping an adequate amount, and getting **E**xercise. **MASTER**y involves engaging in activities that build a sense of competence and accomplishment. These activities need not be major, but they need to be simple enough to build up a client's sense of self-efficacy after they experience a major hit, be it a breakup, illness, or job loss. The following client handout uses this acronym to summarize many of the tools presented in this workbook, and it also outlines additional tools that millennials can use to reduce emotional vulnerability.

Mastering Emotions

Duration: 15-20 minutes	**Frequency:** As Needed	**Level of Difficulty:** Moderate

Instructions: No one ever said navigating life as a millennial was easy. Coming of age in a time of financial uncertainty, high student debt, underemployment, family pressures, and romantic challenges have hit many millennials hard. Already struggling to make ends meet, many in this generation can hit rock bottom over seemingly insignificant (and, of course, significant) life events. It is the old adage of the straw that broke the camel's back. However, unlike the much-more-simplified era from which that wisdom originates, many millennials lack the support that once existed. Whether they are financially strapped or interpersonally isolated, millennials can blow off steam in ways that can be gravely hazardous to their well-being.

The next time you are feeling completely overwhelmed or blindsided by a life circumstance, remember your space of wise mind and how it can help you make healthier decisions in trying times. Tapping into your wise mind can prevent you from making mistakes you may regret later on.

Consider using the acronym **PLEASE MASTER** in helping you stay in a space of wise mind, where you can better protect yourself and reduce emotional vulnerability to hazards down the road. It may help to imagine yourself as the ultimate master of your own emotions and, in turn, your destiny.

> **PL:** Treat **P**hysica**L** illness. As a result of insurance and financial restraints, millennials often avoid going to the doctor or getting a regular check-up in favor of using WebMD® to self-diagnose. Make sure your body is in tip-top shape, as this will also help you navigate life when the going gets tough.
>
> **E:** **E**at a balanced diet. As discussed earlier, minding our plate goes a long way in ensuring healthy, sustained energy levels. Instead of drowning your sorrows in cupcakes, remember to get your fill of fruits, veggies, and proteins. Peanut butter protein smoothie, anyone? Your body and emotions will thank you later.

A: Avoid mood-altering drugs. Pay attention to those wine nights, cocktail times, and happy hours that you might be hitting up a little too strongly.

S: Sleep enough. You learned some sleep hygiene hints in Tool #1, which involve turning off your screens, picking up a good book, and sliding into bed on the earlier side. Make some relaxing herbal tea, take some deep breaths, and relax. Your bed is your new best friend. (Just don't go overboard.)

E: Exercise. Take the time to incorporate 30 minutes of physical activity into your life three to four times a week. Small steps truly do count and make a difference. Look at some of the suggestions provided in Tool #3 to get you started.

Build **MASTERy**: Engage in activities that help you feel competent and confident. This might involve getting back into music, taking a cooking class, or learning a new language. Be open to new experiences, embrace diversity, and seek out connectedness with others. Whatever activities you chose, take the time participate in them with an attitude of mindfulness. You can refer back to the Behavioral Activation Coping Tools List for more ideas. Having a sense of mastery across a number of domains makes it easier to deal with challenging situations.

Finally, make a pledge to yourself on the ways you intend to **PLEASE MASTER** your emotions.

I, _____ on this date_____
               (first name)   (month, day, year)

intend to **PLEASE MASTER** my emotions in the coming weeks and months through the following actions:

_____

_____

_____

_____

_____

Signature _____

Tool #35	Hitting the Panic Button (Distress Tolerance Skills)

THERAPIST OVERVIEW

Frequently, our millennial clients come to us in a state of major distress. They may call it an "emergency" or "crisis"—which, many times, is accurate—but other times, they are simply in a state of frenzy. Of course, once we have done our due diligence in conducting a safety assessment and determining that our clients are safe, figuring out next steps can be challenging. How do we help to calm a frenzied and panicked millennial sitting in our office? Their phone may be going off every 30 seconds, or they may even be in the midst of a live breakup that is unfolding right before your eyes. (More on that in the accompanying tip). Asking your client to simply "slow down" in this situation may not go over particularly favorably either.

In order to help your overwhelmed client, you can introduce them to distress tolerance skills, which originated from dialectical behavioral therapy and are aimed at helping clients cope with difficult situations instead of resorting to self-harm or other dangerous behaviors. For millennial clients in particular, who may have had poor role modeling of healthy coping mechanisms, emphasizing the importance of using these skills is paramount.

One distress tolerance skill that clients can use in times of crisis is "Wise Mind **ACCEPTS**": (**A**ctivities, **C**ontributions, **C**omparisons, **E**motions, **P**ushing away, **T**houghts, and **S**ensations) (Linehan, 2015). The beauty of this skill is multifold. On the one hand, the acronym allows for a good range of diversity in terms of suggested coping tools, and on the other hand, it is easy to implement. Because this mnemonic is easy to remember, it makes it more likely that clients will turn toward this distress tolerance skill in challenging times.

Clients can use **A**ctivities to distract themselves from their current distress and engage meaningfully in anything that can help alter their mood positively, whether it is going for a run or getting a haircut. **C**ontributions can help millennials step outside of their own shoes and care for others in small but impactful ways, whether showing up at a soup kitchen to serve others or helping the neighbor's child with math homework. **C**omparisons align beautifully with an ever-present challenge for millennials on social media, as clients are encouraged to stop making upward social comparisons. Comparing their lives to the rich and famous will only make them feel worse about themselves. By contrast, remembering the struggles they had themselves not too long ago can be a humbling experience.

Working to cultivate positive **E**motions can help millennials get out of their current mental rut and into a better state of mind. Encourage them to watch a movie they love or to do something they know will bring more joy into their lives. While much of therapy often focuses on processing difficulties, there are times when **P**ushing away unpleasant **T**houghts can be the better course of action. Finally, focusing on **S**ensations is an excellent way to help millennials ground themselves in the present moment.

In the section that follows, you'll find two worksheets to help clients put these distress tolerance skills into practice. The first worksheet is aimed at helping millennials understand and implement Wise Mind **ACCEPTS**, whereas the second worksheet focuses exclusively on the **S**ensations aspect of the skill to further provide them some skills around healthy coping.

In-Session Tip:

With the ubiquity of phones in therapy sessions, there may be times when you witness the very challenges your clients have been talking about unfold right in front of you. Maybe an intrusive parent keeps texting their child while you try to conduct the session. Or, perhaps a boyfriend is calling (for the second time) asking where the list of groceries is again. Many times, technology can distract our clients in session, but most fascinating is when these interruptions form the basis of a true immersive type of therapy. I have worked with countless millennials in the various stages of a breakup who have been actively texting (and insulting) their current or ex-partner in the session. Or, they get a sudden text from an old flame and have no idea how to respond. When this occurs, the therapist can wind up in the role of texting coach. This need not be a role to avoid. Embrace it! Encourage your client to share what has been going on, and help them practice the skills you have been discussing. How do they access their wise mind? How might they push away the discomfort of sitting with a text going unanswered? What might be a way to respond to a text in a thoughtful way motivated by kindness and compassion? These are some key learning moments in therapy to be fully explored.

Hitting the Panic Button: Part 1

Duration: 30-40 minutes	**Frequency:** As Needed	**Level of Difficulty:** Moderate

Instructions: The next time you find yourself in need of a panic button, look no further! Don't go to the cupboard and take out the shot glasses, or open up any hookup apps that can lead to headaches and regret later on. Instead, you can get yourself into a place of wise mind through a skill known as "Wise Mind **ACCEPTS**." As any millennial in a state of panic knows, meditation and slowing down may not always be the magic trick you need. You want to forget your worries and find a way out of your latest conundrum. You want a little reprieve, a sense of peace, and an intuitive sense that everything will be alright. The **ACCEPTS** acronym can help you do all of that and more.

The next time you are in a state of distress, instead of trying to escape it or numb out in an unhealthy way, use Wise Mind **ACCEPTS** to not only find a sense of acceptance of the situation, but to allow yourself to become more grounded and mindful in the present moment in a way that won't make you want to run away. Here you'll find an example provided for each letter of the acronym, along with a space for you to fill in an example from your own life to help you start practicing this key skill.

Activities: Distract yourself from difficult emotions by participating in hobbies, exercising, creating art, or listening to music.

Write down an example of an activity you might engage in when you're tempted to numb out:

_____

_____

_____

Contributions: Take your mind off your own worries and concerns by turning your focus and attention to the ways you can help someone else or a cause. For example, you might volunteer for an organization or pet sit for a neighbor.

Write down an example of a contribution you could make when feeling blue:

_____

_____

_____

Comparisons: While social media encourages plenty of unhealthy comparisons, it is sometimes beneficial to compare yourself to people who are coping with difficult emotions as well. Maybe you have a good friend, a trusted older sibling, or a cousin who has experienced similar challenges as you and is coping in positive ways. Comparing your situations and how you can integrate healthy coping tools can help you feel better.

Write down the name of a person or people in similar circumstances and what they are doing that is helping the situation. Then, write down how this can help you work on healthier coping skills:

_____

_____

_____

Emotions: Trying to evoke the opposite emotion of what you are currently feeling can sometimes help you snap out of a funk. Although you do not want to minimize true depressive or anxious feelings, sometimes you might just be feeling blue for no reason at all. Watch a quick, funny YouTube clip you love (being mindful to not numb out on a screen for an extended period of time), turn on upbeat music and dance, or do some cardio to get the endorphins pumping.

Write down what positive emotion you are trying to evoke and what you might do to accomplish this:

_____

_____

_____

Pushing away: Mentally, you might be able to push away unwanted thoughts through a meditation practice where you focus on your breath, say a mantra to yourself, or simply count from one to ten over and over again. When you notice thoughts come up, you might imagine them floating away like clouds in the sky or leaves floating down a river.

Write down a type of imagery that can help you build a wall between you and the intrusive and difficult thoughts:

_____

_____

_____

Thoughts: Distract your mind through activities that require you to think, whether it is reading, doing a puzzle, solving math problems, or memorizing lines from a favorite song.

Write down what type of thoughts might distract you from your challenging emotions:

_____

_____

_____

Sensations: Tuning into your senses can help you if you are tempted to engage in unhealthy coping behaviors. Try holding ice in your hand, taking a warm bath, or smelling a pleasant lotion or essential oil.

Write down one way you can use your senses to help improve the moment:

_____

_____

_____

Hitting the Panic Button:  Part 2

Duration: 30-40 minutes	**Frequency:** As Needed	**Level of Difficulty:** Moderate

To continue practicing and integrating the principles of mindfulness into your daily life, you can further extend the **ACCEPTS** model by focusing in on the final step of the acronym: **S**ensations. Many millennials find that using their five senses can help ground them when they feel overwhelmed and tempted to numb out. The examples that follow suggest how each of the five senses can promote a greater sense of mindfulness and peace. There is also space for you to provide your own ideas.

Sight: One of the most commonly practiced forms of meditation is a candle meditation. It involves focusing on the flame, breathing deeply and calmly, and mindfully observing the flickering movement. Other examples of using sight include taking a mindful walk and just noticing each tree and leaf, and even individual blades of grass.

Write down an example of how you might tune into your sense of sight to practice mindfulness:

_____

_____

_____

Smell: Perhaps the fastest sense to make an impact, our olfactory system is directly tied to our brains, which explains why our memories of smell are so powerful. Whether it is the smell of fresh cookies or newly cut grass, smell can be very instrumental in altering our mood.

Write down an olfactory memory and how you might be able to tune into your sense of smell to boost your mood:

_____

_____

_____

Sound: Whether it is the mesmerizing sound of a piano or beats from your favorite band, sound can immediately transport us by making us feel understood and supported. In contrast to sad music, which can intensify an unhappy mood, upbeat music can have us uncontrollably tapping our feet.

Write down how you might use your sense of sound to help you feel calmer and find more happiness:

_____

_____

_____

Touch: Anyone who has stroked the soft fur of a beloved pet or other animal knows that feeling of warmth and the soft rise and fall of another living creature's breath can instantly make us feel connected to a larger whole.

Write down how you might use touch to feel grounded in the present moment:

_____

_____

_____

Taste: This sense has gotten many of us in trouble, as few things can be as comforting as a giant bowl of ice cream, chocolate, or freshly baked lemon bars. In moderation, though, taste can move us into a space of nourishing our bodies with healing foods.

Write down how you might use your sense of taste to help you feel more present:

_____

_____

_____

Conclusion

Growing up as a millennial in this era has been at times exhilarating, and others exhausting. There is the promise of technological advancements that are life changing and deeply inspiring. However, there is also a freneticism, loss of connection and purpose that is ever looming. Holding an awareness of a delicate balance between lifelong l earning and embracing of new horizons while maintaining our roots and values is more important than ever before. Millennials are truly one of the first generations to experience this firsthand.

Many are postulating that life post mobile phone technology has fundamentally shifted who we are and how we connect (or disconnect) from others. We are at risk for lives devoid of the color and spontaneity that existed before our planned virtual coffee dates. And yet, when used properly, technology is allowing us to create more time and space for family and friends—we are not tethered to our desks and dial-up internet anymore and can truly travel the world and take in so much more life. While ever tiptoeing on the balance beam where we may tilt too far one way or another, millennials possess a deep intuition of when things feel out of balance.

It is hoped that this book is one of many tools and resources that can help millennials and those who care for them come back into a state of equanimity. Hopefully, they take care of their bodies and minds and consider shifting their priorities to find what matters most in their lives. Perhaps this book can help millennials connect more deeply with others, learn to tap into their wise mind, and find time to breathe whether on a bus or while drinking their morning coffee. May this book serve as a treasure chest of sorts with all kinds of jewels and crystals that can help promote better sleep, less anxiety, and much more joy.

There is a reason millennials are making what may seem like drastic decisions—moving into tiny homes so they can be rid of college loan debt once and for all or delaying marriage or having children until they can truly take care of themselves holistically. Whatever stage in life a millennial may be in, it is hoped this treasure chest will serve them throughout their incredible journey and beyond.

References

American Psychiatric Association. (2017, May 22). *Majority of Americans say they are anxious about health; millennials are more anxious than baby boomers.* Retrieved from https://www.psychiatry.org/newsroom/news-releases/majority-of-americans-say-they-are-anxious-about-health-millennials-are-more-anxious-than-baby-boomers

Ballard, J. (2019, July 30). *Millennials are the loneliest generation.* Retrieved from https://today.yougov.com/topics/lifestyle/articles-reports/2019/07/30/loneliness-friendship-new-friends-poll-survey

Benson, L. (2019, August 26). *Social media comparison infographic.* Retrieved from https://www.leveragestl.com/social-media-infographic/

Bocci, G. S. (2012, August 29). 6 steps for finding the right yoga practice. *Psychology Today.* Retrieved from https://www.psychologytoday.com/us/blog/millennial-media/201208/6-steps-finding-the-right-yoga-practice?amp

Bocci, G. S. (2019). *The social media workbook for teens: Skills to help you balance screen time, manage stress and take charge of your life.* Oakland, CA: Instant Help Books.

Borkin, S. (2014). *The healing power of writing: A therapist's guide to using journaling with clients.* New York: W. W. Norton & Company.

Bratskeir, K. (2017, December 7). This is what happens to your body when you text. *Huffington Post.* Retrieved from https://www.huffpost.com/entry/texting-and-health-effect-on-your-body_n_7616022

Chadra, K. (2018, May 8). NSC statement on IIHS report on increased pedestrian deaths. *National Safety Council.* Retrieved from https://www.nsc.org/in-the-newsroom/nsc-statement-on-iihs-report-on-increased-pedestrian-deaths

Cigna. (2018). *2018 Cigna U.S. loneliness index.* Retrieved from https://www.multivu.com/players/English/8294451-cigna-us-loneliness-survey/docs/IndexReport_1524069371598-173525450.pdf

Covey, S. (2013). *The 7 habits of highly effective people.* New York: Simon & Schuster.

de Shazer, S. & Berg, I. K. (1995). The brief therapy tradition. In J. H. Weakland & W. A. Ray (Eds.), *Propagations: Thirty years of influence from the mental research institute.* Binghamton, NY: The Haworth Press.

Duckworth, A. G. (2018). *Grit: The power of passion and perseverance.* New York: Scribner.

Emmons, R. A., & McCullough, M. E. (2003). Counting blessings versus burdens: An experimental investigation of gratitude and subjective well-being in daily life. *Journal of Personality and Social Psychology, 84*(2), 377–389.

Emmons, M. (2018, October 9). *Key statistics about millennials in the workplace.* Retrieved from https://dynamicsignal.com/2018/10/09/key-statistics-millennials-in-the-workplace/

Estes, A. C. (2018, September 4). *My smartphone gave me a painful neurological condition.* Retrieved from https://gizmodo.com/my-smartphone-gave-me-a-painful-neurological-condition-1711422212

Flückiger, C., & Grosse Holtforth, M. (2008). Focusing the therapist's attention on the patient's strengths: A preliminary study to foster a mechanism of change in outpatient psychotherapy. *Journal of Clinical Psychology, 64,* 876–890.

Fox, K. C., Nijeboer, S., Dixon, M. L., Floman, J. L., Ellamil, M., Rumak, S. P., ... Christoff, K. (2014). Is meditation associated with altered brain structure? A systematic review and meta-analysis of morphometric neuroimaging in meditation practitioners. *Neuroscience & Biobehavioral Reviews, 43,* 48–73.

Gallup. (2016). *How millennials want to work and live.* Retrieved from https://www.gallup.com/workplace/238073/millennials-work-live.aspx

Good Therapy. (2019, August 26). *Control issues.* Retrieved from https://www.goodtherapy.org/learn-about-therapy/issues/control-issues

Goyal, M., Singh, S., Sibinga, E. M. S., Gould, N. F., Rowland-Seymour, A., Sharma, R., … Haythornthwaite, J. A. (2014). Meditation programs for psychological stress and well-being. *JAMA Internal Medicine, 174*(3), 357–368.

Hansen, M. M., Jones, R., & Tocchini, K. (2017). Shinrin-yoku (forest bathing) and nature therapy: A state-of-the-art review. *International Journal of Environmental Research and Public Health, 14*(8), 851.

Herosmyth. (2017, June 6). *41 revealing statistics about millennials every marketer should know* [Blog post]. Retrieved from https://www.herosmyth.com/article/41-revealing-statistics-about-millennials-every-marketer-should-know

Kiley, D. (1983). *The Peter Pan syndrome: Men who have never grown up.* New York: Dodd, Mead & Co.

Lamb, T. (2004). Health benefits of yoga. *The International Association of Yoga Therapists.* Retrieved from https://www.iayt.org/page/HealthBenefitsOfYoga

Linehan, M. (2015). *DBT skills training handouts and worksheets* (2nd ed.). New York: Guilford Press.

ManpowerGroup. (2016). *Millennial careers: 2020 vision facts, figures and practical advice from workforce.* Retrieved from https://www.manpowergroup.com/wps/wcm/connect/660ebf65-144c-489e-975c-9f838294c237/MillennialsPaper1_2020Vision_lo.pdf?MOD=AJPERES

Petersen, A. H. (2019, September 9). How millennials became the burnout generation. *BuzzFeed News.* Retrieved from https://www.buzzfeednews.com/article/annehelenpetersen/millennials-burnout-generation-debt-work

Pew Research Center. (2014, March 7). *Millennials in adulthood.* Retrieved from https://www.pewsocialtrends.org/2014/03/07/millennials-in-adulthood/#racial-diversity

Pew Research Center. (2019, February 14). *Millennial life: How young adulthood today compares with prior generations.* Retrieved from https://www.pewsocialtrends.org/essay/millennial-life-how-young-adulthood-today-compares-with-prior-generations/

Raes, F., Pommier, E., Neff, K. D., & Van Gucht, D. (2011). Construction and factorial validation of a short form of the Self-Compassion Scale. *Clinical Psychology & Psychotherapy, 18,* 250–255.

Rubin, G. (2017, February 23). *7 types of loneliness (and why it matters).* Retrieved from https://gretchenrubin.com/2017/02/7-types-of-loneliness

Stairs, A. M., Smith, G. T., Zapolski, T. C. B., Combs, J. L., & Settles, R. E. (2012). Clarifying the construct of perfectionism. *Assessment, 19*(2), 146–166.

Stinson, F. S., Dawson, D. A., Goldstein, R. B., Chou, S. P., Huang, B., Smith, S. M., Ruan, W. J., Pulay, A. J., Saha, T. D., Pickering, R. P., & Grant, B. F. (2008). Prevalence, correlates, disability, and comorbidity of DSM-IV narcissistic personality disorder: results from the wave 2 national epidemiologic survey on alcohol and related conditions. *The Journal of clinical psychiatry, 69*(7), 1033–1045. https://doi.org/10.4088/jcp.v69n0701

U.S. Chamber of Commerce. (2012). *The millennial generation: Research review.* National Chamber Foundation. Retrieved from https://www.uschamberfoundation.org/sites/default/files/article/foundation/MillennialGeneration.pdf

Vogels, E. (2019, September 9). *Millennials stand out for their technology use, but older generations also embrace digital life.* Retrieved from https://www.pewresearch.org/fact-tank/2019/09/09/us-generations-technology-use/

Ward, A. F., Duke, K., Gneezy, A., & Bos, M. W. (2017). Brain drain: The mere presence of one's own smartphone reduces available cognitive capacity. *Journal of the Association for Consumer Research, 2*(2), 140–154.

Recommended Readings

Asatryan, K. (2016). *Stop being lonely: Three simple steps to developing close friendships and deep relationships*. Novato, CA: New World Library.

Bien, T. (2006). *Mindful therapy: A guide for therapists and helping professionals*. Boston: Wisdom Publications.

Bocci, G.S. (2019). *Digital detox card deck: 56 practices to help you detox, de-stress, distract, and discover!* Eau Claire, WI: PESI Publishing and Media.

Brown, B. (2015*). Daring greatly: How the courage to be vulnerable transforms the way we live, love, parent, and lead*. New York: Avery Publishing Group.

Bush, A. D. (2015). *Simple self-care for therapists: Restorative practices to weave through your workday*. New York: W.W. Norton & Company.

Colier, N. (2016). *The power of off: The mindful way to stay sane in a virtual world*. Louisville, CO: Sounds True Publishing.

Davis, T. (2019). *Outsmart your smartphone: Conscious tech habits for finding happiness, balance, and connection IRL*. Oakland, CA: New Harbinger Press.

Douillard, J. (2001). *Body, mind, and sport: The mind-body guide to lifelong health, fitness, and your personal best*. New York: Three Rivers Press.

Gilbert, D. T. (2007). *Stumbling on happiness*. New York: Vintage.

Glei, J. K. (2016). *Unsubscribe: How to kill email anxiety, avoid distractions and get real work done*. New York: PublicAffairs.

Kabat-Zinn, J. (2005). *Wherever you go, there you are: Mindfulness meditation in everyday life*. New York: Hachette Books.

Neff, K., & Germer, C. K. (2018). *The mindful self-compassion workbook: A proven way to accept yourself, build inner strength, and thrive*. New York: Guilford Press.

Pinker, S. (2015). *The village effect: How face-to-face contact can make us healthier and happier*. Toronto: Vintage Canada.

Singer, M. (2015). *The surrender experiment: My journey into life's perfection*. New York: Harmony Books.

Tolle, E. (2004). *The power of now: A guide to spiritual enlightenment*. Vancouver: Namaste Publishing.

Turkle, S. (2017). *Alone together: Why we expect more from technology and less from each other*. New York: Basic Books.

Wisdom, J. P. (2019). *Millennials' guide to work: What no one ever told you about how to achieve success and respect*. New York: Winding Pathway Books.

Made in the USA
Columbia, SC
06 October 2020